Discovering Job

THE GUIDEPOSTS BIBLE STUDY PROGRAM

Floyd W. Thatcher *General Editor*
Robin White Goode *Associate Editor*
Bob E. Patterson *Technical Consultant*

Job

Discovering Job   David L. McKenna
What This Scripture Means to Me   Jeanie Miley
Cover Artist   Ben Wohlberg

DISCOVERING JOB

The Guideposts Bible Study Program

GUIDEPOSTS®

Carmel   New York   10512

The photographs on the pages below were reproduced with the permission of the following photographers:

Bruce Cresson: 27 (*top and bottom*), 37, 71, 117, 142, 159
William La Sor: 44

THE GUIDEPOSTS BIBLE STUDY PROGRAM
The Book of Job
    1. DISCOVERING JOB
    2. My Working Bible
    3. Knowing More About Job

Contents

Publisher's Introduction

With the drama of the Book of Job we are introduced to the first of the Wisdom books in our Bible. Wisdom literature, however, had its beginnings in the antiquity of the ancient Near East. Some of the earliest wisdom literature appeared in Egypt and Mesopotamia between 2,500 and 2,000 B.C. Biblical wisdom literature began to appear on the scene around 1,000 B.C.

Like their predecessors in more ancient times, biblical wisdom writings were styled as proverbs, monologues, dialogues, and debates. They were for the most part lengthy discussions on life's major questions. In addition to the Book of Job, the Books of Proverbs and Ecclesiastes, and some of the Psalms form the corpus of the biblical wisdom writings. However, the influence of the wisdom of the sages is felt in the Song of Songs (Solomon) and the Book of Lamentations as well.

The wisdom literature was styled as poetry, and this is true of the Book of Job except for the prologue, Chapters 1 and 2, and the epilogue, Chapter 42:7–17. To the twentieth-century reader Hebrew poetry may seem quite confusing. The emphasis is on ideas and not meter. It is distinctive for its parallelism—the second line of a couplet repeats the thought of the first line but with different wording. Or, one part of the couplet is positive and the other part is negative. Another distinctive quality of the wisdom writings is their richness in the use of metaphors, similes, parables, and riddles.

Because of the nature of the thinking and writing in the Book of Job, we suggest that in addition to the regular biblical text you follow along as well in two or three modern language versions. We would especially recommend *The New English Bible, The New International Version, The Good News Bible,* and *The Jerusalem Bible.* Any one or all of these should be helpful in illuminating the story and heightening the drama.

The setting for the Job adventure is "the land of Uz." We can't be certain as to the location of Uz, but it was likely somewhere along the trade routes between the Jordan River and the Euphrates River and north of Arabia. Because of the reference of the Lamentations writer, "Rejoice and be glad, O daughter of Edom, that dwellest in the land of Uz" (4:21), some early interpreters associated Uz with Edom, however, this does not seem likely. It is possible that Uz was adjacent to Edom on the east or that at one time the Edomites had occupied Uz.

We are equally uncertain as to when the Job drama was played out. Some Bible interpreters have questioned whether or not Job was an actual historical character. But setting that question aside, the power of the story is unquestioned. The setting for the drama, however, was quite likely timed before the Law was given to Moses on Mount Sinai because early in the story we're told that Job acted as a priest in offering his own burnt sacrifices.

Chapters 1 and 2, the prologue, set the stage for the action and the discussions which make up the major part of the drama. It is here we meet the wealthy family man who feared God and avoided evil. And it is here, too, that we have the tragic tale of how he lost everything and was stricken with a loathesome disease. Finally, it is in the prologue that we are introduced to Job's three friends who, having heard about the calamity, traveled the trade routes to commiserate with Job. And when they arrived they grieved with him in silence for seven days.

Then follow the dramatic and lengthy discussions that took place. The central theme of these dialogues is one that has plagued people from that time until now, "Why do good and upright people suffer?" At the very outset we become aware of the fact that Job's three friends focus on the simplistic position held by even the sages in that ancient time—that all suffering is the result of sin; a righteous person will not only be prosperous but will also not have to go through hard times of suffering. And it is this idea that Job in his intense misery speaks out forcefully against. While he is an upright man and fears God, he doesn't boast of being without sin, but as he sees it, God is causing him to suffer way beyond what he might deserve. He insists again and again that the calamity which has robbed him of everything but life itself is not the result of sin.

Yet, as we proceed along through the Job adventure, we can't help but be moved by his loyalty to God even in the midst of his bewildering hard times and unanswered questions. Yes, he asked questions. And, yes, he argued with God and at times came close to blasphemy. But through it all he remained steadfast in his faith.

As you will see, there are many practical lessons to be learned from the Job story. But there is one especially that we want to underline because it also speaks loudly to us today as we struggle through our Christian pilgrimage. When Job's three friends heard about the tragedies that had ruined him, they traveled long, hard miles to be with him. Then they cared enough to sit in silence with him for seven long days. As so often happens during times of suffering, there aren't words to express the deepest feelings, but just being there is important.

But then when Job broke the silence and expressed the agony he felt, the three friends became judgmental and turned against him. He didn't react according to their formula, and so in their own self-righteousness they lashed out at him, and attempted to bludgeon him into their way of thinking. They failed him miserably in his moment of great need. At the very time Job needed friends to stand by and support him, they were not with him in spirit.

The gift of friendship is one of God's most marvelous serendipities. It is one of the most Christian of our relationships. Being a caring and supportive friend is a powerful Christian witness.

Job isn't mentioned in the "Faith Hall of Fame" of Chapter 11 of the Book of Hebrews. In fact, Job is mentioned just two other times in our entire Bible. The prophet Ezekiel mentions his name along with Noah and Daniel (Ezek. 14), and the writer of the Book of James gives him a well deserved accolade which sums up the central thought in our lessons, "Behold, we count them happy which endure. Ye have heard of the patience of Job, and have seen the end of the Lord; that the Lord is very pitiful, and of tender mercy [Job stood firm and in the end the Lord treated him with compassion and mercy]" (James 5:11).

Preface

To study the Book of Job is an experience of a lifetime. No book of the Bible has as many facets which have been explored by ancients and moderns alike. If we approach the book as a literary classic, it will not fail us. Its theme is timeless, its appeal is universal, its language is matchless, and its moral is eternal. No wonder that such literary giants as Tennyson and Carlyle acclaim the Book of Job as one of the greatest and grandest literary works of all time:

   . . . to the poet, Job is epic verse;
   . . . to the novelist, Job is classic literature;
   . . . to the composer, Job is majestic song;
   . . . to the philosopher, Job is profound wisdom;
   . . . to the playwright, Job is dramatic intrigue;
   . . . to the psychologist, Job is behavioral insight;
   . . . to the theologian, Job is weighty doctrine; and
   . . . to the preacher, Job is sermonic treasure.

Yet, Job's story is intensely personal. It has meaning for every person in every culture in every time. We do not need to be poets, philosophers, psychologists, playwrights, or preachers to understand the book. How else can we explain an ever-increasing interest in the book? Whether it is Archibald MacLeish's Broadway play named "J.B." or

Rabbi Harold Kushner's runaway best-seller with the eternal question as its title, *When Bad Things Happen To Good People* each is based on the Job theme.

In reality every person on earth identifies with Job at one time or another. We long for his disciplined righteousness and his practical wisdom. We weep with him in the tragedies that wiped out his fortune and his family. We scream with him from depths of physical suffering. We rebel with him at the insensitivities of friends upon whom we thought we could count.

We, too, wonder why God is silent just when we need Him most. But then, with Job, we hear the voice of God out of the whirlwind and realize that He has something more for us to learn. When all is said and done, we confess with Job, "I have heard of thee by the hearing of the ear: but now mine eye seeth thee" (42:5). In that confession rests our hope—for physical and emotional healing, for social restoration, and for spiritual redemption.

But we are far ahead of our story. The study of the Book of Job begins with a question, not an answer. In fact, the question we ask about the book determines the answer that we will receive from our study. Satan, for instance, asked the skeptic's question, "Does Job serve God for nought?" In other words, did Job serve God because of the blessings he received? We will learn the answer to that question as we become acquainted with Job and the nature of his faith.

Job himself asked the sufferer's question, "Why was I born?" His question still hangs in the air. We do not understand the reason why God permits suffering, especially among innocent people. Skeptics turn this question into a reason for agnostic and sometimes atheistic doubt. We will not learn the answer to this question from the study of the Book of Job, at least to the satisfaction of skeptics.

God's question to Satan will be our guide. When Satan appears before the Council of Heaven to report on his restless wanderings on earth, God asks him, "Have you considered my servant Job?" A world of meaning is wrapped up in this question. God is not only revealing a personal relationship that He enjoys with Job, but He is also expressing utter confidence in his integrity.

But even a man who is commended as "perfect" in wisdom and righteousness by human standards has room to grow. Therefore, God is also saying that Job can stand the test of his faith at the hands of Satan. Contrary to some opinion, God is not wagering with Satan on Job's destiny of succumbing to Satan's intimidation. He still has Job's welfare in mind when He permits Satan to test him by tragedy. Until we confront the contradictions of life which put our faith to the acid test, we do not become the mature believers God intended us to be.

This is the story of Job. Introduced to us as an example of human righteousness, Job is remembered as an example of God's grace. In between, he is tested by tragedy, debate, reflection, criticism and revelation. In each case, Job's response contributes to his growth toward grace—whether in an angry yell against God, a bitter retort against his friends, a sullen silence under criticism, or a subdued confession of sinful pride.

Job's story is our story. His tests are our tests. His reactions, however, may or may not be our reactions. If we are skeptics, we may react to testing with bitterness and perhaps blasphemy. If we are believers, we will still react at first, most likely with the skeptic's question, "Why?" But if we will not let God go, He will eventually speak to us. When He does, it will be in the form of another question, "Who am I?" Once we see who He is, we will drive deeper the stake of our commitment so that the tether of our faith can play out to cover the contingencies of human existence, including the question, "Why do the innocent suffer?" When we know Who God is, the question "Why?" is the stimulus to spiritual growth rather than skeptical disbelief.

Discovering Job is a journey—literally the Pilgrim's Progress of the Old Testament. It is a struggle with spurts, a path that leads through swamps to mountain peaks, a tragedy with some comic relief, but always an adventure that moves us forward to the time when we bow before God, receive His grace, and become all that He intends us to be.

I invite you on a journey with Job. Markers for the journey come as lessons that will keep us moving toward the goal of our study—to share Job's trust in God and receive God's grace for us.

LESSON 1
JOB 1:1–5

Introducing Job: Example of Righteousness

Father, Help me to grow in righteousness as I read and study Your Word. AMEN.

To understand Job we must know about the land in which he lived, the school of religious thought to which he belonged, and the quality of life which he exemplified.

Each of us is a product of the time, place, and culture in which we live. Think, for example, about living in the *time* one hundred years ago. Our nation struggled in the transition between the Age of Agriculture and the Age of Industry. Most people lived on farms or in villages, few enjoyed the benefits of higher education, and none knew the impact of electronic media or the threat of nuclear annihilation.

Today, by contrast, our characters are shaped by the influences of an industrialized, urbanized, bureaucratized, and commercialized nation. Furthermore, we are educated, affluent, mobile, and diverse. Our tastes are dominated by the media, and our values are influenced by the secular mind. The time in which we live makes the difference in how we think, what we believe, and who we are.

The Land of Uz (1:1)
The Time

The Place

Think also about the *place* in which we live. As a person who has lived in the Midwest, the Northwest, and the South, I am particularly conscious of regional differences that shape our attitudes and values.

As a boy growing up in a small town in the Midwest, I remember how social pressure stratified people. Religion is a good example. I remember classifying the kids in high school who didn't eat meat on Friday as Roman Catholics. The Lutherans drank beer and the Baptists didn't dance. The Episcopalians were Catholics who had flunked Latin.

Later in life we moved to Seattle, Washington. My Midwestern religious mind was shocked to find that church attendance there was the lowest in the nation, denominational differences lacked intensity, and religious beliefs crossed over all the lines of social strata. Yet, when tested for spirituality, I found Northwest people as strong in their convictions, if not stronger, than their Midwestern counterparts.

One day as I was driving down a steep hill in Seattle, Washington, a view of the whitecaps on Puget Sound and the white peaks of Olympic Mountains opened before my eyes. Then and there I felt as if I had discovered the difference between the flatlands of the Midwest and the rugged mountains and seas of the Northwest.

The environment where we live tends to shape and reinforce our character. In the Midwest, people tend to cluster in towns and cities as groups with strong social pressure. But in the Northwest, a pioneer spirit persists in which persons are identified as individuals more than as members of a social group, an ethnic culture, or a denominational affiliation.

The Culture

Culture complements the time and place in which we live. By definition, culture is the attitudes, beliefs, values, and customs which are unique to a civilization, a nation, a community, or an institution.

Six years ago, our family made another transcontinental move, this time from the Northwest to the South. Shock waves went through our souls again as we encountered the bedrock tradition of the South in contrast to the rugged individualism of the Northwest. When we redecorated the President's Home at Asbury Theological Seminary, for instance, we chose soft and neutral colors rather than the more formal Williamsburg blues. When an interior decorator heard our ideas, she sniffed, "Oh, you want California style!"

The heavy weight of Southern tradition hit us full-force when we attended our first University of Kentucky football game. To open the season and the game, the former Governor of the state stepped up to a microphone and sang, "My Old Kentucky Home." His voice cracked from the weight of emotion when he reached the phrase, "Weep no more my lady . . ." I looked around the stadium to see scores of Kentuckians caught up in the swelling tide of emotion, dabbing at their eyes and singing through their tears.

At that moment my mind raced back to my earlier years in Michigan. Vaguely, I remembered singing "Michigan, My Michigan" but only as a necessity at a formal function. My thoughts then leaped forward to my adult years in the state of Washington. Not once do I remember singing the official song of the state. In fact, I don't even know the name of the song. Yes, indeed, the culture in which we live has a profound effect upon the shaping of our attitudes, values, tastes, and aspirations.

The Time of Uz (1:1)

Job is introduced to us simply as a man who lived in the "Land of Uz." Believe it or not, a wealth of meaning is contained in this simple fact. Uz is a shadowy land of the ancient past. We know little about its time, place, and culture except from bits and pieces of archeological evidence in the biblical record.

However, Uz is a real place, not a fantasy. As to the times it existed, we know that the Land of Uz is so ancient that it predates written history. Sometime after Adam's banishment from the Garden, Noah's building of the Ark, Abraham's journey by faith from Ur of the Chaldees, and the captivity of the children of Israel in Egypt, there was a man named Job who lived in the land of Uz. As vague as the dating may seem, we know that Job lived *before* God revealed His written Law to Moses on Mount Sinai and before He established the nation of Israel as His chosen people.

The Religion of Natural Revelation

Timing is crucial to understanding the Book of Job because it means that he had no special, written revelation to guide him in his search for God. We who have the benefits of Holy Scripture, church history, Christian theology, and literally millions of religious books can hardly imagine what it would be like to pursue our thirst for God without special, written revelation. Yet, we must try to put ourselves in Job's time. He had only the *natural revelation* of God's creation to guide him.

As I write, I have the advantage of an outdoor setting that I would nominate as the eighth wonder of the world. Lake Chelan, in the state of Washington, is a snow-packed body of water that snakes out of the Cascades mountain range for fifty miles until it drops over Chelan Falls into the Columbia River. The sky is blue, the sun is hot, the clouds are cottonballs, the breeze is fresh, and the mountains stand serene on each side.

For me, all of the majestic beauty of God's creation comes into focus at Lake Chelan. But before the day ends, we can expect the Chelan wind to come whipping down the lake, raising whitecaps and endangering every foolish sailor who fails to heed the warning. When the wind comes, the awesome power of God's creation will overwhelm its beauty. Still later when the wind dies and the water is calm, we will watch the sun go down over the Western mountains and realize that the scene will survive long after we are gone. The mountains are symbols of eternity. They, too, will pass away, but their age and strength points us to the eternal nature of God who has no beginning, no end, and no shadow of turning in between.

Creation Reveals God

Natural revelation also showed Job the majestic beauty, awesome power, and eternal nature of God. Throughout the Book of Job these themes are expressed time and time again. Job and his friends sing of God's majestic beauty, quake before His awesome power, and bow before His eternal nature. The Book of Job vouches for the truth that we can know God through natural revelation.

Prophetically, the Book of Job confirms the Apostle Paul's statement in his letter to the Roman Christians. In speaking to the question about the spiritual fate of people who do not have the advantage of the special revelation of the Scriptures he wrote, "For the invisible things of him from the creation of the world are clearly seen, being understood by the things that are made, even his eternal power and Godhead; so that they are without excuse" (Rom. 1:20).

These words of the great Apostle give us the essence of religion based upon natural revelation. In nature we see evidence of the Person and power of God. And it is these truths, as elementary as they seem, that form the foundation for Job's religion.

The Place of Uz (1:1)

The introduction of Job as a man who lived in the Land of Uz also gives us some vital facts about *the place* in which he lived. Although our knowledge of the Land of Uz is severely limited, we do know that it was located somewhere to the east of the Jordan River. In ancient times, the Jordan River marked the dividing line between the civilized and uncivilized worlds.

To the west of the Jordan River lay the cities of culture, commerce, education, and religion. To the east lay the untamed frontier—hazardous on all counts—desert waste with its capricious weather, vicious beasts, and roving bands of land pirates.

Only the most daring of adventurers sought their fortunes in the land east of the Jordan River. Like the wild and woolly West of American history, the Land of Uz symbolized the wild and woolly East of ancient history. Job lived in a lawless land in which fortunes were made and lost overnight due to the whimsical weather, ruthless thieves, and vicious competition.

The Culture of Uz (1:1)
Home Centered

Another fact crucial to our understanding all that follows resides in the four-word phrase, "The Land of Uz." We know that a land which predates written history and lies to the east of the Jordan had a patriarchal society in which the father represented the

The broken lines indicate the major highways or caravan trade routes of the Ancient East. The major east-west route began at the northern tip of the Persian Gulf on the east, moved northwest through Ur and Babylon, and then divided with the eastern branch threading its way up the Tigris River to Nineveh and other centers. The western branch continued northwest to Aleppo where it then headed south to the coast and on to Egypt.

Connecting routes branched off along the way to Haran, Carchemish, and Tarsus. At Damascus the King's Highway headed south, east of the Jordan River, to Elath. From Elath a branch moved its way south along the eastern shore of the Red Sea while another branch made its way west to Egypt.

While we cannot locate the land of Uz, it is likely it was located east or southeast of the King's Highway, but west of the Euphrates River. In Genesis 36:28 and Lamentations 4:21 Uz is identified with Edom. It is possible Uz was located east of Edom but at various times was occupied by Edomites. Job in all probability lived on or near one of the major trade routes. This would have enhanced his commercial activities and would also have made his camp readily accessible to his three friends who traveled along the trade route from the East to visit him.

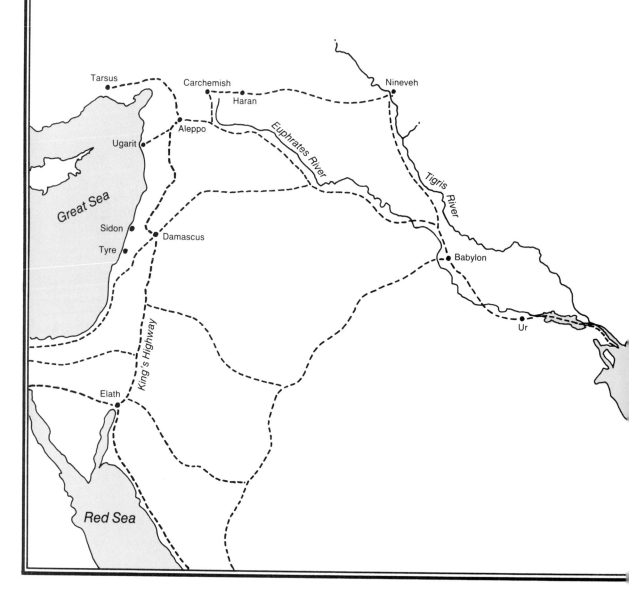

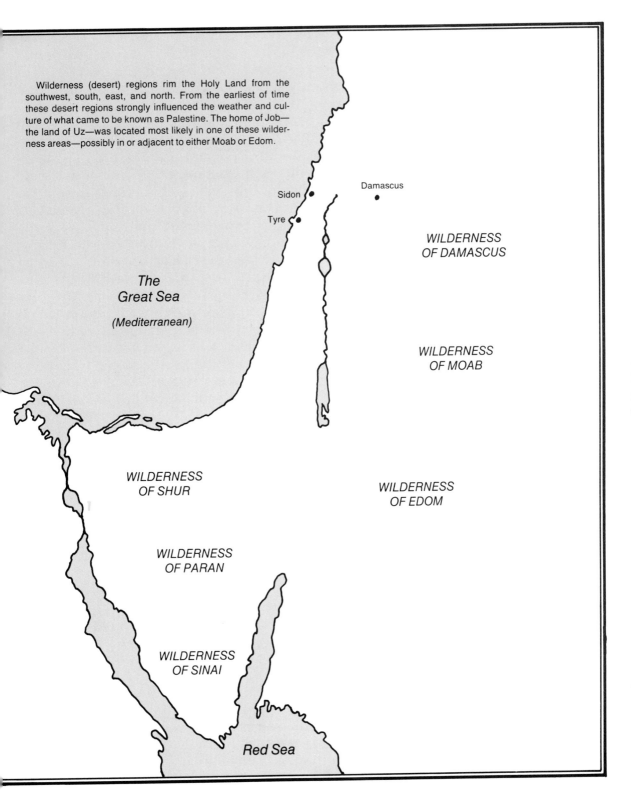

Wilderness (desert) regions rim the Holy Land from the southwest, south, east, and north. From the earliest of time these desert regions strongly influenced the weather and culture of what came to be known as Palestine. The home of Job— the land of Uz—was located most likely in one of these wilderness areas—possibly in or adjacent to either Moab or Edom.

Sidon

Damascus

Tyre

WILDERNESS OF DAMASCUS

The Great Sea

(Mediterranean)

WILDERNESS OF MOAB

WILDERNESS OF SHUR

WILDERNESS OF EDOM

WILDERNESS OF PARAN

WILDERNESS OF SINAI

Red Sea

institutions of the home, church, school, government, and business. Spiritually as well, all of the culture centered around the home, and the male head of the house served as the prophet, priest, and king for the entire family.

This kind of a culture is strange to us today. We live in a time in which the absolute authority of the father has been broken and his role in the family is shared with other institutions outside the home. While there are disadvantages in concentrating so much power in one person, there are also advantages.

In modern society, wherever the functions of the family are taken outside the house one set of problems is traded for another. Day-care centers, for instance, assume the role of parents in caring for children. Yet the evidence comes in that day-care children do not learn the social graces and spiritual values which only caring parents can provide. Day-care children tend to sharpen their values against their peers who are also two-, three-, and four-year-olds. Even in the best day-care centers, surrogate parents cannot replace the modeling, supervision, and love of the mother and father. Especially in spiritual development, there is no substitute for the parent and the role of the father.

Hero of the Culture

Every great civilization has an image of the ideal person. Critics of late twentieth-century society say that that is our problem. We have no heroes that represent the ideals of our time. When young people are asked to name the people they most admire, celebrities from the fields of rock music, professional sports, and violent movies are named first. Except for their special talents, however, these heroes are only bits of persons. Frequently their personal lives are a mess, their characters are repulsive, and their aspirations are selfish.

Job is just the opposite. He is introduced to us as a total person who represents the most advanced ideals of his time, place, and culture. While no person is perfect, Job comes as close to perfection as anyone we meet in the Old Testament. In a very real sense, we can think of him as a person who points us forward to the Person of Jesus Christ—our ultimate example.

We are introduced to Job as a man who was "blameless and upright," "fearing God" and "shunning evil." Each word has meaning.

In his heart, Job was "blameless." No duplicity plagued him. He was one of those rare people who harbored no hate nor covered no sin at the center of his soul. While he himself will later admit that he is not sinless by nature, nevertheless, he can claim to be "blameless" in the motives of his heart.

Job is as "straight" in his outer behavior as he is "blameless" in his inner desires. My use of the word "straight" refers to an unswerving plumb line of behavior. Again, Job is a rare person—we always know where he stands, and we can always count on his actions.

I have a dear friend who is a perceptive student of human behavior. After studying the success of religious celebrities who attract millions of loyal followers with one basic speech, he told me, "I have figured out their success. Wherever and whenever you find them, they are never out of role." More sophisticated studies of effective leaders confirm his observation. Consistency is a quality which prompts people to trust their leaders.

While Job's consistency of behavior is an asset we admire, his highest commendation is the integrity of his character. "Blameless" and "straight" tell us that he is the same man inside and out. Most of us nurse hidden flaws of character which we try to cover by rigid external standards. The tension catches up with us when we live under the fear of discovery.

Just this week I visited with a man who enjoys an outstanding reputation as a Christian leader in his community. He is known for his conservative standards and his compassionate self-giving. When I was with him in a casual setting, however, a stranger rubbed him the wrong way. Sparks flew from his lips as he reduced the man to ashes with the fire of his tongue.

In contrast I have another friend, who is the chair-

The Righteousness of Job (1:1)
Blameless in Heart

Straight (Upright) in Conduct

Consistent in Character

23

man of a large corporation. Puzzled by the relaxed setting of his corporate office from which multi-million dollar decisions are made, I asked him, "How do you handle stress?" With a soft and knowing smile, he gave me his answer, "As long as I am the same man inside and out, I have no stress." Job would join him in his conclusion. If we are "blameless" in our hearts and straight or upright in our behavior, stress is the least of our worries.

The Wisdom of Job (1:1)
The School of Wisdom

We have seen Job as the epitome of righteousness. He is also the epitome of wisdom. Thinking in the ancient East was dominated by what was called the Wisdom School, made up of scholars and students who tried to know God and live righteously through the revelation of natural creation.

Motivated by their intense hunger for God, the Wisdom School thinkers exercised their gift of human reason to reflect upon nature, formulate their beliefs, and teach others their faith. As we have already inferred, their creed centered on a belief in a sovereign God whose awesome power created the physical universe and all forms of life, culminating in the creation of rational and spiritual human beings.

The observations of the Wisdom School thinkers led them to draw connections between the events of nature. Natural law became evident as they witnessed cause-and-effect at work in the creative order. This meant that if they obeyed the laws of nature, they survived and prospered, but to defy those laws meant destruction and death. So, they concluded that God's awesome power is matched by His immutable justice. Transferring this conclusion into the human realm, they then developed a doctrine which prompted them to live a life of disciplined righteousness. Taken directly from the principles of cause-and-effect in the natural order, they reasoned that righteousness brings prosperity, and *vice versa,* sin results in suffering.

Before we write off the Wisdom School for formulating a negative religion, we must remember that their ideas still persist today. Many people are attracted to versions of Christianity that promise prosperity. Distortions abound when the Scripture proof text is quoted, "Seek ye first the Kingdom of God, and His righteousness; and all these things shall be added unto you." Then, too, which of us does not ask about our sin whenever we suffer? The Wisdom School is still with us.

The Source of Wisdom

At the same time we have to give the Wisdom School credit. Motivated by their thirst to know God and activated by their ability to think about God, they set wisdom as the goal for their spiritual quest.

By definition, wisdom is the ability to see things whole. Consequently the discipline of righteousness was not an end in itself. Nor did it represent just a cowering before the power and justice of God. By worship and righteousness, they hoped to understand the ways of God in the world and His purpose for humankind. In their search for God, Wisdom School people leaned into the future when God would lift the veil on His special revelation—the written Law of Moses, the promise of the prophets, and eventually the coming of Jesus Christ. Beginning with the power of God, then, and leaning toward His promises, the Wisdom School people put their faith into the capsule of a single sentence, "The fear of the Lord is the beginning of wisdom" (Psa. 111:10).

Fearing the Lord

Job personifies the Wisdom School. We have seen the integrity of his inner and outer life in righteousness; we now see the integrity in his vertical and horizontal relationships. Vertically, he "feared the Lord."

Fear of God may be negative or positive. We can be paralyzed by fear before the awesome power of an angry God, or we can bow and worship before the majestic power of a loving God. As we will see throughout our study, Job's "fear of the Lord" is based upon a reverential relationship with a God who is at one and the same time the untouchable sovereign of the universe and the intimate friend with whom Job walked and talked.

Shunning Evil

Another hint about Job's relationship with God comes to us in his horizontal relationship with the world in which he lives. Because he feared the Lord,

Job also "shunned evil." Fear is a weak motivation for shunning evil in the long run. We need a higher motivation for morality. Of course, as the Apostle Paul reminds us, love is the greatest motivation of all. He wrote, "the love of Christ constrains me." So we can infer that Job's fear of the Lord went beyond fright to respect and worship, even love. In that sense, he approached perfection in wisdom as he began to see things whole.

The Fame of Job (1:2–3)
A Perfect Family

Our introduction to Job continues with the description of his family, his fortune, and his fame. Perfection abounds once again, at least in human terms. According to ancient standards, Job had the perfect number of children—seven sons and three daughters. Seven symbolized "wholeness" to the ancients and in a patriarchal age, seven sons represented "perfection." In turn, three daughters rounded out the family and left nothing to be desired. Note also the priority of Job's family in the listing of his wealth. His children came ahead of his possessions. Job is my kind of man.

A Perfect Business

The numbering of Job's possessions is not accidental either. "Seven thousand sheep, three thousand camels, five hundred yoke of oxen, and five hundred donkeys" reveal the abundance of his wealth (1:3). The numbers of sheep, camels, oxen, and donkeys are all "perfect" for the area and the time.

Ranchers, traders, farmers, and builders set their goals at these numbers, and when they reached them, they knew they had arrived. But Job went one better. By achieving the "perfect" number in diverse fields, he became a large multinational corporation with many companies of note. His sheep filled the hillside, his camel caravans plied international trade routes, his oxen ploughed acres and acres of farmland, and his donkeys carried sand and stone, wood and mortar for construction. To top it all off, Job had so many servants that the head count is lumped into the phrase, "a very large number of servants."

Greatest in the East

To summarize Job's family and fortune, the author of the Book of Job flatly states that he "was the

From the beginning of recorded history flocks of sheep like
those pictured above have roamed the rugged countryside in
the vast wildernesses between the Jordan and the Euphrates
rivers. We're told that Job had "seven thousand sheep"
among his vast herds.

27

greatest of all the men of the east." How significant! In the wild East with its treacherous environment, its lawless nature, and its unstable culture a good and godly man stood head and shoulders above all others. A single word in our Scripture lesson tells us why. Job's righteousness is related to his riches and his reputation by the word, "And" (Job 1:2). The relationship is not necessarily a matter of cause and effect, but it is a matter of conjunction—meaning that Job held his righteousness and riches in balance—one complementing the other.

At every turn Job amazes us. His life is a model, not only for his day, but for ours as well. Few of us can hold righteousness and riches in balance. One either spoils the other or we pursue one to the neglect of the other. Job teaches us that the quality of our character and the integrity of our life makes the difference.

The Fatherhood of Job (1:4–5)
A Celebrating Family

Righteousness, riches, and reputation are empty without quality in human relationships, especially with our families. Job qualifies as "perfect" on this count too. Our Scripture lesson tells us that his family knew how to celebrate. We're told that his sons took turns holding feasts in their homes and even inviting their sisters to eat and drink with them (1:4).

Happy families know how to celebrate. As a boy, I remember looking forward to holidays when my father's family came together. Everyone brought food to share, but to me the fun extended far beyond the feast. My uncles always had projects on which they were working—a model railroad, a sailboat, an electronic system. I stood in awe of their genius, especially when they let me help.

Then after dinner came the stories. Our family history unfolded for me in the laughter of tales about our ancestors. But the day never finished without games. I still remember my ecstasy as a boy when my mother let me stay up until midnight learning how to play Monopoly.

One day, though, marital conflict struck deep at the heart of our family. At the last family reunion I attended, tension killed our joy. Husbands came late and left early. There were no projects, stories, or games. Even the food lost its taste. Still, I retained my early love for family celebration. In our home, we put a premium upon holidays, celebrating birthdays, inventing family rituals, making specialty foods, and creating devotional symbols that will never be forgotten.

But Job's family had a special sense of celebration. The fact that the seven sons of Job invited their three sisters to celebrate with them is an act of love, not necessity. Unfortunately, women had little worth in the patriarchal age of Job's time. More than that, the Land of Uz was a man's land in which brute strength was most highly prized. We understand, then, why the Scriptures make special note of the relationship between Job's sons and daughters. Even though their father was dominant in the household, he taught his sons to value their sisters as persons, not possessions. Only a father could communicate those values.

A Loving Family

Job's family also knew how to worship God. Without a synagogue or a priest, Job accepted his responsibility as spiritual head for his family. How sensitive he was to their needs. Although celebration can often lead to excesses that can lead to sin, the Scriptures tell us that Job's children did not sin in their feasting. Still, the temptation persisted, so Job took it upon himself to make sacrifices for his children just in case they sinned and "cursed God in their hearts" (1:5). What a marvelous example of spiritual nurture. Before they sinned, Job regularly prayed and offered sacrifices for his children. Unfortunately, many of us pray for our children only after they have sinned, when it is too late, or in crisis.

A Worshiping Family

Probably no person in Scripture other than Jesus Himself is more thoroughly examined than Job. Yet under the microscopic eye which magnifies his righteousness, his riches, his reputation, and his relationships he remains blameless in his heart, straight in his conduct, reverential in his worship, and strong against evil. Without the special revelations of Scripture, the commandments of the Law, the promise of the Prophets, or the redemptive grace of Jesus Christ,

Job is "perfect" in righteousness for his time, place, and culture.

How do we improve on perfection? The multiple tests of suffering were yet unknown to Job. On the sacred journey ahead, we will learn that his "perfection" is relative. Even Job has room to grow. And so do we.

Father, Help me to be like Job, who was a disciplined person of prayer. AMEN.

WHAT THIS SCRIPTURE MEANS TO ME
Job 1:1—5

It was the perfect setup. Marian and Joe had been to all the "right" schools and were superbly equipped for their professions. They had researched carefully to find the community that could offer them the best quality of life, and now they were set in the house of their dreams, going about the business of the good life.

Following their well-ordered goal-setting, the Fredericks had their children just when they planned them and made sure that they were in the "right" school district and carpools. Their family joined the "right" clubs and found the "right" church.

Marian and Joe were savoring the American dream of the good life, carefully tending the hedge about their lives and working hard to keep misfortune or problems away from their door. After all, they had covered all the bases with their sound and sensible planning; life wouldn't cave in on them as it had for some of their friends.

"Work hard," was their watchword. "Keep up appearances," and "Take care of your own backyard," were other messages they gave to each other and, now and then, to friends who didn't quite have their patina of perfection polished to the same high gloss. Living well seemed so easy, if only you would do the right things.

The Old Testament contains the record of an earlier, "perfect" family. The Job writer describes a man who was "perfect and upright and one that feared God and eschewed evil." Scripture says that Job was "the greatest of all the men in the east." By all appearances, he had it all together.

Things haven't changed so much since Job's time. We humans still spend our days and nights trying to neatly arrange the circumstances of our lives in an orderly fashion. We want things to come together according to our plan. And in our pride we forget that anything we place before God in our affections is bound to disappoint or destroy us.

Time was when I bought into the fantasy that if I could do enough, have enough or be enough, I could avoid pain or problems. Somehow, I believed that if I did all the right things, I was entitled to good health, a comfortable wealth, and a stress-free life.

Like the Fredericks, I took a lot of pride in my independence and self-sufficiency. I didn't have to ask for anything or depend on anyone else to help me (or so I thought), but could take care of myself in almost any situation. I could even handle God by going to church. I knew where I was going, and what I was going to do when I got there!

Bombarded by advertisements, I assumed that because there was a remedy or a pain-killer that would work instantly for whatever ailed me, I wasn't supposed to feel any discomfort. The subtle message I got was that if I did hurt, an instant fix would be the answer. Soon, I came to believe not only that I wasn't supposed to hurt, but that I couldn't stand to hurt, if, for some mysterious reason, pain were to strike.

I have given up those fantasies now, however, and I have a few scars here and there to show for the process. In giving up my innocence and naivete, I have gained a little wisdom, for I have come to see that if you live long enough, life will happen to you.

Whether it is through a major calamity or through a slow-growing hunger that cannot be satisfied by education, power, success, or money, the need for God eventually surfaces. Either because of an external happening or an internal dis-ease, each person eventually comes up against his own inability to make something work. Each of us ultimately faces, in one way or another, the impotence of the false gods we have fashioned for ourselves.

"The only thing you need to know about God is you ain't he," proclaims the down-home philosophy. I need to hear that now and then so I won't forget who is really in charge.

LESSON 2
JOB 1:6–3:26

The Test of Tragedy

Lord, Even in the tragedies of my life, let me see Your love and power. AMEN.

Some people seem to lead a charmed life. They possess natural abilities which we envy, succeed in whatever they do, and enjoy life to its fullest. Job appears to be that kind of person. Although we know nothing about his early life, we suspect that he was born right, grew right, and lived right until the time we meet him in his maturity. Later writers might have commended him as they did Jesus when Luke writes "And Jesus increased in wisdom and stature, and in favor with God and man" (Luke 2:52).

Job is introduced to us with the same commendation. He is almost too good to be true. Yet there is a missing dimension of his life. He has never learned to suffer. His perfection, however, sets the stage for a new reality. Will Job's goodness stand the test of tragedy? As the prophet Jeremiah reminds us, it is one thing to run with footmen, but how will we do in a horse race? Or it is one thing to dwell in the land of peace, but quite another to survive when the Jordan River swells (Jer. 12:5). Job has yet to experience this kind of adversity.

The Missing Dimension

The Council of Heaven
(1:6–12)

The scene temporarily shifts in our Scripture lesson now from Job on earth to God in heaven. In an insightful glimpse into heaven, our setting has God in session with all the hosts of heaven, and it is reporting time. Suddenly God spots an intruder among His angels. Satan, himself, has come home. Certainly His heart must have hurt when Satan at an earlier time had rebelled against Him so violently that God had no choice but to cast him out of the heavenly court along with a third of the angels.

Contrasting Spirits

We don't catch any hint of threat in God's words as He asks Satan matter-of-factly, "Whence comest thou?" In response Satan answers, "From going to and fro in the earth, and from walking up and down in it" (1:7). Contrasting spirits are in this scene. God is calm and confident; Satan is restless and insecure.

Those who deny the existence of Satan will be hard-pressed to explain this heavenly episode. But, even for those who might believe that Satan is not real, his restless, wandering spirit cannot be denied. It is far more realistic to recognize the existence of evil in a personal form that preys upon our souls. Whoever wrote the Book of Job had the same view of Satan as being the essence of evil as Peter the Apostle did when he described Satan as a ". . . roaring lion, [who] walketh about, seeking whom he may devour" (1 Peter 5:8).

The Smile of God

God accepts Satan's answer and then asks him, "Hast thou considered my servant Job, that there is none like him in the earth, a perfect and an upright man, one that feareth God, and escheweth [shuns, avoids] evil?" (1:8). Obviously, Job's reputation has reached to heaven. In fact, God goes far beyond the human commendation which identified Job as "the greatest man among all the people of the east."

From God's point of view, Job is one of a kind on earth. Again we realize that no human being, other than Jesus Christ, received such acclaim by God. We also realize that Job's righteousness went beyond a discipline based upon fear. When God asks Satan

"Hast thou considered My servant Job?" He reveals a relationship of love and pride which is possible only between friends. As Abraham was called God's friend because he believed in Him (James 2:23), the same might be said of Job. He was God's friend as well as God's model for righteousness on earth.

The Sneer of Satan

Satan's answer to God's question betrays his true character (1:9–11). His words are loaded with sarcastic skepticism. Satan has nothing good to say about anyone or anything.

The most miserable people I know are those who turn everything good into criticism. I have an acquaintance who cannot stand to be outdone. No matter what someone says, she has the superior answer. No matter how successful someone is, she can put them down. Five minutes in her presence and you want to run for your life.

But Satan is far worse. When God commends Job as one of the most noble of people, Satan quashes His enthusiasm by impugning Job's motives. With a demonic sneer, he scoffs, "Doth Job fear God for nought?" (1:9). There is just no way that Satan can understand a spiritual relationship in which Job loves God for His own sake, not for the blessings He bestows upon him.

Why Serve God?

Still, there is a sting for each of us in Satan's question. How would we respond if asked, "Why do you serve God?" Deep down, we must confess that our motives are mixed. We may be like the man who converted to Christianity, Judaism, Islam, and Buddhism all at the same time because he wanted to make sure that he covered all the bases.

Our motive for serving God may also be based on a mingling of guilty fears, earthly blessings, and eternal protection. God understands, but He longs for so much more from us and for us. As Jesus summed up the greatest commandment of all, "Thou shalt love the Lord thy God with all thy heart, and with all thy soul, and with all thy mind, and with all thy strength . . . [and] Thou shalt love thy neighbour as thyself" (Mark 12:30–31).

While these words speak of a commandment, we

are talking about a relationship more than a commandment. As God is love, He desires love as the essence of His relationship with us. Only love explains why He created the universe; only love explains why He created us in His own image with the dignity, creativity, and freedom to make our own choices. If God has a need, it is for us to love Him for Who He is, not for what He does for us.

The Gall of Satan

Next, Satan presses his case by challenging the integrity of God, "Hast not thou made a hedge about him, and about his house, and about all that he hath on every side? thou hast blessed the work of his hands, and his substance is increased in the land" (1:10).

Only Satan could speak with such unmitigated gall. God, not Job, is now the victim of his venom. Satan is saying that God, to win the love of His human creatures, has to curry their favor by protecting and blessing them.

But immediately after questioning God's integrity, Satan challenges Job's integrity, as he says, "But put forth thine hand now, and touch all that he hath, and he will curse thee to thy face" (1:11).

Reckless readers of the Book of Job see God and Satan in a contest of egos with Job as the innocent and helpless pawn. But if that were the case, the spiritual meaning of our story would be lost. Then the Book of Job would become nothing more than another betting game between two jealous and equal gods who manipulate humans for their own purposes.

The Confidence of God

Nothing else in the Book of Job supports that kind of a view of God. Not even Job in the worst moments of suffering entertains such a distorted idea. Instead, we are to interpret this scene as an expressive picture of God's utter confidence in Job. Knowing Job as He does, God is willing to lift His hedge of protection around His servant's life in order to demonstrate the essence of their relationship.

It is important for us to understand at this point that God does not take Satan's challenge to strike at

Job's possessions. God didn't do that then, and He doesn't now. He does permit the attacks of Satan in the accidents of nature to afflict His people. We know, of course, that Christians are no more exempt from suffering than non-Christians. In fact, Christians may be more vulnerable because of their sensitivity.

In the next scene of the Job story we learn that God releases Satan to take away everything that Job has, but with the limit that he cannot touch Job's life or health (1:12). Our confidence in a caring God rises as we read the Lord's words. Perhaps we take for granted the hedge of protection God puts around our lives and the blessings of possessions that He gives to us. At the same time, we can be assured that He will not let Satan push us beyond our limits or destroy us. We can bank without question on the eternal truth in Paul's promise to the Christians in Corinth, "God is faithful, who will not suffer [allow] you to be tempted above that ye are able; but will with the temptation also make a way to escape, that ye may be able to bear it" (1 Cor. 10:13).

When tragedy struck Job, his goats, sheep, cattle, and servants were completely wiped out. Pictured here are goats, sheep, and cattle like those Job lost.

Four Catastrophies (1:13–19)
Natural Accidents and Human Evil

It is at the outer limits, though, of our hard times and suffering where our faith is truly tested. And now we see that Satan pushes on those limits by engineering four catastrophic events which wipe out all of Job's possessions—his herds, his caravans, his servants, and his children.

Let's move in for a closer look. It was on a feast day of high celebration, that a messenger came to Job with the tragic news that a roving band of Sabeans from southwestern Arabia had rustled his herds of oxen and donkeys and killed his servants (1:14–15).

Then, before the first messenger had finished speaking, another breathless survivor of catastrophe arrived to announce that lightning, vividly described as the fire of God, had "fallen from heaven [the sky]" and had struck and killed all the sheep and their shepherds. Next, a third messenger arrived with the bad news that an organized army of Chaldeans had surrounded Job's caravans, stolen his camels, and killed their drivers and keepers (1:16–17).

But there's more—while still reeling from blow after blow, one more messenger arrives and gives Job the most tragic news of all, "Thy sons and thy daughters were eating and drinking wine in their eldest brother's house: And, behold, there came a great wind from the wilderness, and smote the four corners of the house, and it fell upon the young men, and they are dead; and I only am escaped alone to tell thee" (1:18–19).

The Test of Catastrophe

Both natural accidents and human evil serve Satan's purpose in testing Job by catastrophe. The lightning which is described as "the fire of God fallen from heaven" and the tornado which crushed Job's children are so-called "acts of God" which we cover by insurance today. But in truth, they are the random acts of nature which cannot be prevented or controlled.

The Sabeans, however, were helter-skelter land pirates of evil intent who lived by plunder and died by violence. This was not the case, though, of the Chaldeans who stole Job's camel caravans. They represented an organized army of a nearby nation whose foreign policy called for the elimination of competition.

So we see that when God lifted His hedge of protection from around Job's life, his sheep and children became innocent victims of natural accidents. But when Satan took the offensive for the cause of evil, he had no trouble finding evil in people and nations to do his bidding.

Job's Response to Tragedy (1:20–22)

We are not told about Job's reactions to the tragic news until the messenger told him about his children's death. Then, however, we see his raw agony as he plunged into deep and intense mourning (1:20). And out of his grief he cried, "Naked came I out of my mother's womb, and naked shall I return thither: the Lord gave, and the Lord hath taken away; blessed be the name of the Lord" (1:21).

His words astound us. How can a man face the loss of all that he loves and still praise God? Yet, these are the same words that we hear at the graveside when our loved ones die. Somehow, someway, we find strength to bear catastrophic losses. Sometimes we even reach nobility.

In the disastrous Palm Sunday tornado which wrecked havoc across Indiana and Michigan sometime during the middle 1960s, psychiatrists expected the mental hospitals to be filled with people who suffered the loss of everything they owned and loved—property and family. Instead, admissions to mental hospitals during the next six months were cut in half. Not only were people able to cope with natural disaster, but in the crisis they began helping others.

Don't Blame God

Job, too, withstood the shock of the natural disasters that wiped out his family and his fortune. Through his mourning he reaffirmed his faith in God; and contrary to Satan's skeptical expectations, he "sinned not, nor charged God foolishly [with being unreasonable]" (1:22). Most of the time we aren't guilty of blaming God for unexpected tragedy. We may wonder why we or our loved ones are the victims of natural disaster or human evil—why bad things happen to good people—but we don't seriously accuse God of being the author of what happened.

The Spirit of Praise

Something more than gritty courage or faithful acceptance was behind Job's response and reactions. Rather than assuming that he had an inherent right to God's blessing or that he had earned God's favor with his own work and righteousness, Job was grateful for all that he had been given and for the time he'd had to enjoy his blessings. In his words here, he thanked God not only for what had been given him but also for the privilege of having had them.

To be able to thank and praise God in time of catastrophic loss requires the maturity of faith that comes only after mourning. Yet, after people who lose family and fortunes work through their grief, a sure sign of healing is their ability to thank God for the memory of their blessings. The loss is just as great and the pain is just as deep, but out of it all emerges a unique statement of faith.

Heaven's Council: Second Session (2:1–6)

As we read this part of our Scripture lesson, we see that Satan does not know how to blush. Rather than being embarrassed by his failure with Job, he brashly reappears "before the Lord" (2:1). He is asked the same question as before, "From whence comest thou?" And Satan responds as he did the first time, "From going to and fro in the earth, and from walking up and down in it" (2:2). Then God asks once again, "Hast thou considered my servant Job?" (2:3). This time, however, God added, ". . . and still he holdeth fast his integrity, although thou movedst me against him, to destroy him without cause" (2:3).

God Suffers Too!

These last words of God to Satan are utterly amazing. While He can never be the origin of evil or a partner in the ruin of His creation, still, God was accepting responsibility for Job's tragedies. But there may be a deeper meaning here. Is it possible that God is so identified with Job that He participates personally in the suffering of His servant? Love is like that. Just today I had to make the decision to let my son drive 2,500 miles across the country with a college friend. While I gave him permission to go, I asked that he call home each night to assure us of his safety. If anything happened to him, my response would be the same as God's. Love lets him go and holds him at the same time.

To better understand God's response, compare His words with Satan's curse. Not a shred of remorse or responsibility is heard as the Evil One lashes out, "Skin for skin, yea, all that a man hath will he give for his life. But put forth thine hand now, and touch his bone and his flesh, and he will curse thee to thy face" (2:4–5). In other words, Satan is saying that a person will give up most anything in the interest of staying alive, but when body and life is threatened, that is another matter—"he will curse thee to thy face" (2:5).

Satan's Curse

Satan's retort exposes the true nature of sin. It is pure, unadulterated selfishness. Satan cannot believe that Job might have loved his children as much as his own life. But, he assumes that Job will do anything to save his own skin.

With this kind of argument, Satan never loses. He only retreats into a rationalization for his defeat in order to attack again. We make a fatal error when we assume that a victory over Satan sends him off with his tail between his legs. Keep this picture of Satan in mind—his primary objective is to go "to and fro in the earth"—roam back and forth across the earth—looking for unsuspecting souls he can destroy. Such singleness of purpose gives him an intensity of focus and a persistency of action which preys upon our mixed motives, uncertain minds, and unsteady steps.

Satan's Persistence

We remember that even in the case of Jesus the temptation in the wilderness at the beginning of His ministry did not defeat Satan. He came back to Jesus again and again with subtle variations on his original temptations to physical gratification, social status, and material wealth. And it was in the Garden of Gethsemane that Satan put Jesus through the ultimate test. Would He give up His own life in abject shame in order to save people from their sins? Not until Jesus sacrificed Himself was Satan defeated. Still, because God permits Satan to exist and work within limits, the Tempter levels every weapon in his arsenal at our selfishness—the center of our morally corrupt nature.

Condemned to the Ash Heap (2:7–10)

Next we see that God's confidence in Job holds steady. He is willing to let Satan test Job at the center of his soul, with one condition. His life must be spared (2:6).

Losing no time, Satan afflicts Job with "sore boils from the sole of his foot unto his crown" (2:7). The man who cut a healthy, handsome, and honored figure in all the ancient Near East is suddenly reduced to a scratching and scraping hulk of scabby flesh on an ash heap. Whether it is the physical pain or the social disgrace, the seriousness of Job's disease is pictured in living color by his wife's reaction, "Dost thou still retain thine integrity? Curse God, and die" (2:9).

Loving Wife or Satan's Mistress?

Critics have maligned Job's wife for centuries. Judgments on her have ranged from the lack of faith in her husband to being the Devil's handmaiden. But I think she deserves better. Satan has a way of using those who love us most as his instruments. Our spouses, for instance, become so closely identified with our destiny that when we suffer, they suffer.

Job's wife dared to ask the question that had to be in her husband's mind. If something is the result of sin as was taught in the Wisdom School, then, surely the grotesque nature of his disease had to raise questions about his integrity. It is more likely, though, that her statement reflects the hopelessness of Job's disease and his ultimate disgrace of being confined to an ash heap outside the city. Rather than see her loved one suffer that kind of agony and humiliation, out of love for him she suggests that he curse God and die as a way out of his suffering. Given the same circumstances, what would we say?

The Stigma of Suffering

Job has fallen from the pinnacle of human greatness to the pit of social disgrace. Because of the stigma of his disease, his lot in life is reduced to an ash heap outside the protection of the city walls.

Each generation has infirmities that it does not
know how to handle. In our day, stigma is attached
to AIDS, aging, anorexia, and Alzheimer's disease.
AIDS, of course, is the worst. With the threat of
becoming an epidemic that could wipe out millions
of people, our fears border on hysteria.

In the heavily afflicted San Francisco Bay area, for
instance, doctors and nurses who are competent pro-
fessionals still feel as if AIDS may be contagious by
contact. Extra precautions are taken even for routine
treatment. A victim of AIDS, particularly one who is
innocent of sexual promiscuity or drug abuse, would
know how Job felt—quarantined as contagious,
shunned by friends, ridiculed by enemies, and diagnosed as terminal—no death is more cruel.

Without Hope of Eternal Life

At least from our vantage point as Christians we
have the hope of eternity. Job had no such hope.
Natural revelation gives intonations of eternity, but
not of eternal life. The life cycle of plants and animals, for instance, includes conception, birth,
growth, maturity, and death, but not eternal life. So,
for the students of the Wisdom School of Job's time
who drew their theology from nature, there was absolutely no hope for life after death. They believed
that at death the human soul departed to a land of
shadows without personal existence. Job clung to life
because he had nothing for which to die.

Three Genuine Friends (2:11–13)

When news of Job's misfortune reached his three
friends, Eliphaz, Bildad, and Zophar, they made
plans to visit him before he died. Usually these three
men are castigated as erstwhile friends and merciless
comforters. But nothing is farther from the truth.

Significant cues in Scripture inform us that Eliphaz, Bildad, and Zophar lived in distant separate
cities. Because messages were scratched like graffito
on signposts at intersections where camel caravans
travelled, the mail was notoriously slow and uncertain.

It must have been months before Job's three
friends heard of his plight. Still more time, perhaps
weeks and months, passed before they made contact

with each other and arranged to meet at a common point in order to travel together and visit their friend. Let's face it, how many friends do we have who would go to the same lengths to visit us? So, rather than prejudging Eliphaz, Bildad, and Zophar, we should honor them as the kind of friends whom we need and want in our hard times of suffering.

A Cause for Mourning

The devastating nature of Job's disease is pictured vividly when we learn that his friends didn't even recognize him as they approached the ash heap. Having seen Job in all his glory as the greatest man in the East, they were shocked to see his robe in shreds, his face disfigured, and his seat of honor turned into a mound of ashes. With the stench of death in the air, Eliphaz, Bildad, and Zophar joined Job in his mourning—tearing their own robes and tossing ashes over their own heads (2:12). For them, Job was as good as dead, and as good friends, the least that they could do was share in his death watch.

They stayed beside him for seven days and seven

In traveling from their homes Eliphaz, Bildad, and Zophar would have traversed through rugged wilderness terrain like that pictured below. This gives us some idea of their feelings of friendship for Job.

nights of silent mourning (2:13). But then their legalism overruled their friendship. Having done their duty, they arose to leave, but Job reacted immediately. Even though he was skating on the edge of death, he was far from dead.

Never Give Up

If you want to be a friend, never give up a person for dead. As long as there is the slightest sign of life, there is hope. A friend of ours struggled with the decision to take the life-support system away from her father, who suffered a stroke that left him with irreversible brain damage.

After months of nonrecognition, she and her sister felt clear before God to make the fatal decision. As the doctor disconnected the apparatus, however, she whispered to her father, "Now, Daddy, you can go to be with Jesus." For the first time in six months, a tear appeared in the corner of his eye and ran down his cheek. Immediately, the doctor reversed his action, reconnected the machines and left our friend with the dilemma of renewed hope.

The Cry of Suffering (3:1–26)

Have you ever wished that you had never been born? Job plummeted to these depths after seven days of horrendous suffering when his friends respected his pain with the comfort of silence. Sometimes silence is the most eloquent language we can speak in the presence of excruciating pain. To force the sufferer to talk only adds to the agony. Personal presence is quite enough. To the credit of Job's three friends, they were sensitive to his needs, not with the comfort of sound, but with the comfort of silence.

Why Was I Born?

Finally, Job couldn't take any more: no more pain, no more shame, no more silence. The patience for which he was known ran out. With a shriek that pierced the desert air, he cried out and cursed the day that he was born (3:1). As if he could turn back time, he wished that he could darken the day and wipe out the night of his birth (3:2–10). Once these words came out of his mouth, Job's bottled-up feelings gushed forth like water from a fire hose as he asked the question "Why?" time and time again, "Why died I not from the womb?" (3:11) . . . "Why the

45

breasts that I should suck?" (3:12) . . . "Or as an hidden untimely birth I had not been; as infants which never saw light?" (3:16).

Why Can't I Die?

With poetic fervor, Job envisions death as peace from his pain, rest from his turmoil, and freedom from his captivity. Job sees death as the great equalizer in which the small and the great, the wicked and the weary, the king and the slave are as one—in peace, at rest, and free.

Why Isn't Life Fair?

Job's cry goes even deeper as he continues to ask "Why?" No longer is he cursing the day of his birth; now he is questioning the fairness of life for those who suffer intolerable physical, emotional, and spiritual pain. He seems to be asking, Why is life given ". . . to him that is in misery?" (3:20) . . . "unto the bitter in soul?" (3:20) . . . "which long for death, but it cometh not?" (3:21) . . . "to man whose way is hid?" (3:23).

Why Not Mercy Killing?

Issues of abortion and euthanasia are not new. Job is raising questions about the beginning and the end of life. In effect, he is saying, "If we know the suffering which a baby will go through later in life, isn't it merciful to neglect or abandon the child?"

For contemporary medicine, the question is real. If a seriously handicapped child is born who is condemned to suffer until early death, should extra measures be taken to keep the child alive? Or at the other end of the life spectrum, if a person is hopelessly ill and longs for death, should life-saving treatment be continued? The gravity of these questions illustrates the despair of Job. Of all men, he is most miserable.

Sooner or later, each of us faces the same circumstances. It is some comfort to know that a person as good as Job asks our questions for us. But our greatest hope rests in the fact that Jesus, Himself, when He confronted the intolerable pain and the utter shame of the cross, He, too, asked God, "Father, if it be possible, let this cup pass from Me."

Job's distress has not yet robbed him of his hope, but he is close. In a pitiful summary of his suffering, he speaks of "sighings [that] cometh before I eat" and "roarings [groanings] . . . poured out like the waters" (3:24). Then he dared confess that what he feared and dreaded had come upon him (3:25). The peace, quietness, and rest which he enjoyed during his days of glory are gone. All is now turmoil—literally the churning of the soul (3:26).

By admitting that he feared and dreaded the day when he might lose his health, wealth, family, and fame, Job is brutally honest. Underneath the peace and prosperity that so many of us enjoy, the same fear and dread lurk and trouble our night hours. Perhaps we feel guilty about our blessings. Certainly, we know that we don't deserve them. But most of us cannot confess our fears and dreads. They expose too much of our soul. As in Job's case, his honesty will cost him dearly. In his question "Why?" his friends hear a shout against God and in his confession of dread and fear, they sense the guilt of sin.

Almighty God, You know the things that concern me. Thank You for allowing me to entrust them to Your care. Amen.

WHAT THIS SCRIPTURE MEANS TO ME
Job 1:6–3:26

We had been to the mountaintop that morning, high in the Rockies, where the grass is short and the air is thin. Later, our guide took us far down into the valley where wildflowers lit up the landscape and wildlife frolicked. Mountain streams, few and far between in the high country, gained momentum in the valleys, rushing life to the abundant flora.

Our guide was a Vietnam war veteran, lean and limber and given to long silences. Filled with potential and possibilities, he had entered adulthood with all he would need to make life work for him. Now, with the course of his life changed by the choices of war, he was carving out a new path for himself.

Smoke from the hibachi danced slowly around us in the cool Colorado evening. While our guide presided over the cooking, he recalled his travels since the war; whatever had happened during the war would remain buried somewhere deep inside him.

"You know," he said quietly, "one of the things I brought home from Nam was a knowledge of my own strength."

We waited, shivering in the mountain twilight, struck by the power in the silence between us. Gently, he turned the meat over and then gazed off into the mist of evening.

"I didn't want to go to the war. What I saw and heard and smelled and felt was too terrible for words. I didn't think I could stand it. But I survived, and in surviving, I learned I was strong. Nobody can take that away from me."

Those words hovered over me the rest of my vacation, and now and then they haunt me with their implications. Astounded by what I have witnessed others endure, I wonder how I would hold up under the torture of war.

How would I survive in a solitary cell? How would I deal with pain? How would I wear disfigurement or disease? Stripped of everything that had given me security and meaning, how strong would I be? Would I, as Job had done, "fear God for nought?"

I beg God to give me faith. I ask Him to help me learn how to trust, and now and then, when I'm not thinking, I ask Him for patience. I want His strength and I beg for His favors and blessings. I want the joy of His presents; sometimes, however, I don't want to be bothered with His presence.

If I'm honest, my behavior tells the truth, and the truth is that I mostly want a "lite" faith—a faith that doesn't cost me dearly. I cannot bring myself to echo Job's question to his wife: "Shall we receive good at the hand of God and shall we not receive evil?"

It's easy to be swayed by prosperity theology and blessing beliefs: If I believe hard enough, God will bless me with prosperity and good things. It is easy to fall into the trap of thinking that my good works will protect me from the agonies and struggles of life.

The means through which I obtain the strength of a mature faith, however, may not be what I want. It may be that the way I will receive the grace and mercy for which I long is through a time or experience of testing, and that testing may come at the point of my greatest strength.

I have learned now that the God who has come to us through Christ knows exactly where to place the refining fire. He knows precisely where the need for pruning is. He knows how to make me strong, strong enough to withstand the testing of life.

In the midst of the battle, God is there all the time, even when I don't know it. And He is asking over and over, "Do you trust me?" How I respond is crucial.

LESSON 3
JOB 4:1–14:22

The Test of Creed

Lord God, Let the teachings of this lesson be real to me. In Jesus' name. AMEN.

Violence creates violence. With his surprising curse against the day of his birth, Job violated all the protocol of the Wisdom School. Through the measured steps of human reason, "wisdom" represented an attitude as well as a perspective. And calm, cool, and collected reflection characterized the attitude of wisdom.

A wise person never panicked because reason served as the moderating influence and wisdom covered all contingencies. We understand, then, why Job's three friends reacted so violently to his hysterical outburst. As the man who exemplified the ideals of wisdom, his reaction contradicted everything he had taught and everything for which he had stood.

Eliphaz Begins His Response (4:1–6)
The Wisdom of Age

Whenever any school of thought is threatened, someone must come to its defense. And that is what happens now in response to Job's outburst. According to the debating process of the ancient Wisdom School, persons spoke in order of their age because age and wisdom were interlinked. Maturity of thought and breadth of experience are essential elements of wisdom—seeing things whole—and in Job's time, people deferred to age.

Seniority required that Eliphaz be the first to answer Job's intemperate cry of anguish. With an air of reluctant disdain, Eliphaz responds to Job, and his impatience is obvious as he frames his opening question, "If we assay to commune with thee [If we risk responding to you], wilt thou be grieved [lose patience]?" (4:2).

Then like a father scolding a child, Eliphaz reminds Job that his reaction to what has happened to him contradicts everything that he had taught and counseled with others (4:3). And, as if to add insult to injury, Eliphaz then reminds Job that the moment he experienced reverses and suffering, he became discouraged and dismayed and was a poor model for his own teaching.

Undoubtedly Eliphaz had touched a raw nerve, but he pressed on. Using the rhetorical question as his weapon, Eliphaz suggested that if Job were truly pious, he would be calm in his confidence and if he were blameless, he would not give up hope (4:6).

Then as Eliphaz continued to lecture Job, he builds his case by citing three sources of his authority as a man of wisdom—reason, intuition, and experience. Each of these is highly personalized and extremely difficult to refute.

Eliphaz is a master of classical debate. Rather than coming directly to his point, he dances around the subject until he has covered every angle. Then he drives home his point.

The dance begins when Eliphaz invokes the authority of reason. Exercising the prerogative of his senior position, he asks Job to ponder this question: "Who, being innocent, has ever perished?" (4:7). Then playing heavily on the personal authority of his age and reputation, Eliphaz says, "Even as I have seen [as I have observed]." Job knows exactly what his friend is saying because he had spoken those very words time and time again.

Seniority Speaks

The Authority of Eliphaz (4:7–5:7)

The Authority of Reason

Laying claim to a logical process that leads to an indisputable conclusion, Eliphaz puts the premise, ". . . they that plow iniquity and sow wickedness, reap the same" (4:8). For the Wisdom School thinkers this is a fundamental doctrine—sin produces suffering. To reinforce his point, Eliphaz refers to the law of nature in which even a lion, the king of the beasts, is broken despite his roar and growl (4:10–11). Job, the "lion of Uz," gets the point. Even he is not exempt from the law of justice.

The Authority of Intuition

Under ordinary circumstance, Eliphaz might have rested his case at this point. But he knew that Job could always counter reason with reason. So, he proceeds now with colorfully descriptive language to tell Job that he has had a revelation from God. And this revelation came during a midnight visitation from a ghostly spirit who whispered to him with a hushed voice, "Shall mortal man be more just than God? shall a man be more pure than his maker?" (4:17).

As indirect as these two questions may seem, Job understands what they mean. Eliphaz is saying that Job cannot play the innocence game, for he is a sinner by nature who has been crushed by suffering and is in danger of dying without wisdom (4:18–21).

Eliphaz has maneuvered Job into a cleverly designed box. After all, it is hard to argue with a secret word, a gliding spirit, and a hushed voice—even today!

The Authority of Experience

We see next that beneath his fatherly advice, Eliphaz has a mean streak. With a belligerent note, he defies Job to appeal to the holy ones of either the past or present (5:1), for they won't hear him. And he follows that up by once again condemning Job for his violent outburst, "For wrath killeth the foolish man, and envy slayeth the silly one" (5:2).

In one sentence, Eliphaz, for all practical purposes, has excommunicated Job from the Wisdom School. To be called a fool is to condemn him as a person who no longer fears God, is devoid of wisdom, and is doomed to destruction.

Then, to press home his point, Eliphaz invokes the authority of experience once again by saying, "I have seen the foolish [a fool] taking root. . . ." (5:3). With these words Eliphaz pulls rank on Job by stressing his age and experience by inferring that Job fits neatly into a pattern he has seen many times before. And he is saying that it is the consequences that count. Cataloging the consequences of a fool, Eliphaz then reviews Job's losses for him—his home, his children, his harvest, and his wealth. In so many words he is telling Job, "Don't blame the laws of accidents of nature. The reason for your suffering lies within you"—"Yet man is born unto trouble, as the sparks fly upward" (5:7). As you can see, Eliphaz is stressing the ancient idea that our hard times of suffering are caused by what we are and what we have done.

By invoking the authority of reason, intuition, and experience, Eliphaz feels as if he has finally reprimanded Job for his outburst and firmly reestablished the teachings of the Wisdom School. Job is suffering because he has sinned. And, furthermore, he has lost his fear of God.

Secure in his conclusion, Eliphaz now becomes solicitous. We can almost hear the paternalistic inflection as he counsels Job, "I would seek unto God, and unto God would I commit my cause" (5:8).

How quicky Eliphaz changes his tune. The rest of his speech is a beautiful hymn of praise to the goodness of God. Prosperity is promised to the righteous (5:8–11). The wicked are frustrated (5:12–14), and the poor will receive justice (5:15–16).

A beatitude follows. Eliphaz presumes to know why Job suffers, "Behold, happy is the man whom God correcteth: therefore despise not thou the chastening of the Almighty" (5:17).

Rising to his full stature as the eldest and wisest of the three friends, Eliphaz believes that his arguments are conclusive. He leaves Job no recourse but to apologize for his intemperate outburst, repent of his sin, and accept God's discipline in order to be restored. Now, he concludes his speech by invoking all of the authority of his esteemed position, "Lo this, we have searched it, so it is [because of our study and experi-

The Council of Wisdom (5:8–27)

Fatherly Advice

A Word from the Wise

ence, you can be sure that's the way it is]; hear it, and know thou it for thy good [listen to me because what I've said is the truth]" (5:27).

Job's Cry for Help (6:1–18)

In spite of Job's outburst and Eliphaz's speech chiding him for his intemperance, the climate is still relatively calm. Job's response to Eliphaz is to ask that his friends understand the reasons for his feelings.

First and foremost, Job pleads for them to share with him in the depth of his suffering: "O that my grief were throughly weighed, and my calamity laid in the balances together [If my anguish and heartbreak could be weighed on scales]! For now it would be heavier than the sand of the sea [They would outweigh the sands of the sea]" (6:2–3). These words give us a colorful and first-hand picture of the extent of Job's feelings.

Second, he pleads with them to understand why he has asked God to let him die. At least he would have the consolation of knowing that he had died without denying "the words of the Holy One." As strange as it seems, Job sees death as the joy that would make bearable his unrelenting pain (6:10).

Then follows another plea for understanding as Job tries to explain to his friends why he has no hope, "What is my strength, that I should hope? and what is mine end, that I should prolong my life?" (6:11).

With an almost brutal honesty that is characteristic of Job, he admits that he has used up all of his strength and hope for living and has no power or ability to help himself (6:12–13).

Although Job's outcry borders on hysteria, we see in his explanation the laserlike focus of a disciplined mind. As someone once said, "Attendance at your own hanging wonderfully clears the mind." The threat of death clears the mind as well as a hanging.

At one and the same time, Job's outburst of anguish was as thoroughly logical as it was emotionally explosive. We know that the key to understanding the logic of an emotional response is to understand the circumstance out of which it rises. Psychologists tell us that our responses must be appropriate to the stimulus.

In Job's case we have to ask—was the intensity of his outburst appropriate to the depth of his pain? But as we listened to Job's words, we see that he believes his anguish justifies the outrage seen in his response. In fact, he goes one step farther and argues that honesty requires such a response. So, to counter the reasoning of Eliphaz, he defends his reaction as evidence of his integrity, not of his sin.

Job's Bitter Charge (6:19–30)

The more Job tries to explain the intensity of his feelings and his violent outburst to his friends, the more baffled and defeated he seems to feel. It is possible that while trying to explain himself another stab of excruciating pain riddles his body once again. Or he may see bitterness reflected in the eyes of his friends as they listen to him. For we now hear him lashing out unmercifully at his friends for their calloused response to his suffering. And as with most of us, in such moments of frustration, he was guilty of overkill, "To him that is afflicted pity should be showed from his friend [one's friends should be loyal in times of trouble]; but he forsaketh the fear of the Almighty [even if he has turned his back on God]" (6:14).

What Are Friends for?

Talk about a test of friendship! Job puts their friendship on the line by the implied question, "Who's more important, the doctrine or me?" His question echoes down through every generation of history. Jesus had to face that question in His confrontation with the Pharisees. And He was crucified for violating their ritualistic rules.

Even today, we engage in religious "witchhunts" in which people are sacrificed to a dogma of faith, usually one that is a human interpretation of biblical truth rather than the faith itself.

Most of us at times have felt the chill of rejection in a social setting when our theological position, denominational affiliation, political party, or stand on moral issues does not pass the "litmus test" of inquiry from a stranger. I still remember the dinner setting in which I hosted a prominent Christian author. As the evening progressed, he discovered the differences in our theological background. One by one the dominoes of our differences fell until he began to use the term "disillusioned Christians" in such a way that no doubt remained—he meant me.

Dry Streams in the Desert

Job scolds his friends for their insensitivity to his suffering. An eloquent word picture makes his charge most vivid. He likens them to desert streams that overflow in the winter and spring, but dry up in summer when they are most needed. Pathos surges through Job's heart as he compares himself to camel caravan drivers travelling across the desert in anticipation of an oasis in which their thirst will be quenched. Instead, when they arrive, they find only a dry river bed (6:15–20, compare with a modern translation for clarity). At the same time, counting upon the support of his friends when he came to his time of need, Job now says, "For now ye are no thing [you aren't any help to me]; ye see my casting down, and are afraid [you see my condition and are afraid]" (6:21).

Sarcastically, Job reminds them that he never begged favors from them. All he needed and wanted was their understanding. And that really is what being a friend is all about.

Eyeball to Eyeball

Next, though, Job's mood shifts, as in a milder tone he makes himself vulnerable to his friends. Always willing to learn, he says, "Teach me, and I will hold my tongue: and cause me to understand wherein I have erred" (6:24). But at the same time he appeals to them to accept his complaint, however rash, as honest. "Look at me" he urges them. In the land of the East, the eyes are identified as the sensors of the soul. Particularly in delicate relationships of business and government, negotiators sit eyeball to eyeball. No blink of deception, flash of anger, or hint of fear goes unnoticed. By his challenge, "Look at me," Job puts his honesty to the eyeball test. He desperately wants—as we all do—to be understood.

Job's Loss of Hope
(7:1–21)
What Is Man?

As Job continues to wrestle with his loathesome and desperate condition, he asks the question that consciously or unconsciously plagues us in our times of suffering—"What is man?" His immediate response takes on a pessimistic note as he ponders his "months of vanity [futility]" (7:3). Looking down, he sees himself "clothed [covered] with worms and clods of dust" (7:5), and his "skin is broken [scabbed] and become loathsome" (7:5).

From Job's point of view, life is hard (7:1), life is short (7:6), and life is futile (7:9–10). With that outlook, he sees himself as a person with nothing to lose, so he will continue to ventilate his anguish and his bitterness (7:11), but with a difference. Having given up on his friends, Job takes his complaint directly to God, and once again asks, "What is man?"

Out of the emptiness of his own soul Job challenged God with these words, "What is man, that thou shouldest magnify him? and that thou shouldest set thine heart upon him [Why should You consider him important]? And that thou shouldest visit him every morning, and try [test] him every moment?" (7:17–18).

Where Is God?

Indirectly, by asking these questions, Job is chiding the all-powerful and all-knowing God for playing games with His creation. Then, almost as if he was involved in a lover's quarrel, Job says, "How long wilt thou not depart from me [won't you look the other way], nor let me alone till I swallow down my spittle [and leave me alone to swallow my spit (probably an ancient Eastern saying)]? [If] I have sinned; what shall I do unto thee [how does that hurt You], O thou preserver [watcher] of men? Why hast thou set me as a mark [target] against thee, so that I am a burden to myself [to thee]? And why dost thou not pardon my transgression, and take away mine iniquity [why don't you pardon my sins and remove my feelings of guilt]?" (7:19–20). We see in these words the cry of a desperate man, one who longs to be reassured by God. Job was not aware of any transgression that could have brought on his deep trouble, but we catch a hint here that he is beginning to wonder whether he might be guilty of some wrong.

Then, Job even dares to tease the Lord like a jilted lover, as he reminds God that he will die. And when that happens, a deep and abiding relationship that is precious to both God and Job will be broken—God will search for him and miss him when he is gone (7:21).

Bildad's Appeal to Tradition (8:1–22)

Next, Job's second friend Bildad speaks. He is far less patient than Eliphaz, which perhaps reflects their difference in age and position. There's an angry tone to Bildad's comment that was not present in the speech of Eliphaz. To open further the chasm that is developing between Job and his friends, Bildad begins by labeling Job as a bag of blustery wind (8:2). And he then proceeds to defend the justice of God. In a most simplistic restatement of the doctrine of justice, he asks, "Doth God pervert judgment? or doth the Almighty pervert justice?" (8:3)

An Unkind Cut

Perversion is a twist of truth. To Bildad, any variation from the idea that sin produces suffering is perversion—a cruel statement at a time like this. But, Bildad's cruelty is not limited to an explosive outburst. He goes on then to attack Job at the point of his deepest hurt and loss—the death of his children. The idea being expressed (8:4) is that Job's sons were sinners, even as Job is, and their death is proof of God's justice.

After cutting Job to the quick by speaking of his dead children, Bildad's angry tone seems to soften as he comes out with the gratuitous promise that if Job would repent of his sin, whatever it was—if he would become "pure and upright"—God would forgive him and give him peace and a prosperity that would exceed what he'd had before (8:6–7).

Then, to establish authority for what he is saying Bildad betrays his traditionalist mind-set by invoking the thinking of wise men of the past—"consider what the fathers have found" (8:8). Without overworking our imaginations too far it sounds as if Bildad, in an effort to appear profound, is trying to identify himself with wise men of the past and their sayings (8:8–10). This is a favorite ploy even today with speakers and writers whose experience is limited and who, to offset their own lack of experience and knowledge, quote profusely from the sayings and writings of people out of the past like Thoreau or Emerson or Calvin or Wesley.

Bildad then draws three specific parables from wise men of the past to illustrate his beliefs on the doctrine of justice (8:11–19)—a withering reed (8:11–13), a fragile spider web (8:14–15), and a rootless plant (8:16–19). Each of these, Bildad points out, is doomed to destruction because of some internal weakness. His inference is glaring, for he is driving the point home that Job's suffering is due to the sin in his life that is finally exposed. In other words, what has happened to Job is, to Bildad, proof of God's justice.

Parables of Secret Sin

Bildad uses another old technique in his attempt to prove that Job is wrong. He sandwiches condemnation between layers of promise and praise. Having already promised a future that would exceed everything he had known before if he repented and became pure and upright (8:7), Bildad wound up his speech by painting a utopian picture of Job's future, "Till He fill thy mouth with laughing, and thy lips with rejoicing [full of laughter and joy]. They that hate thee shall be clothed with shame; and the dwelling place of the wicked shall come to nought [your enemies will be shamed or disgraced and disappear]" (8:21–22). In today's language, if Job "shapes up" he'll be happy and everything will be smooth.

Flowery Promise and Empty Praise

As an executive who must exercise discipline at times, I find myself using the "praise-criticism-praise" sandwich when I am cowardly. Presumably to soften the blow of confrontation and save face for the person, I will begin and end with a word of praise. But I've decided it doesn't work that way because most people see through the ruse. It is far better to confront the problem decisively and propose ways of recovery than to use empty praise as a means of wiggling out of responsibility. As with me in such moments, Bildad betrayed the uncertainty of his position and the cowardice of his character by trying to cushion his condemnation with flowery promises and empty praise.

Job's Futility and Faith (9:1–10:22)

The dialog between Job and his friends is now going around in circles. In responding to Bildad, Job agrees that what his friend has said is true. And he affirms his own belief in the doctrine of justice. But the question still remains, "How should [can] man be just with God [righteous before God]?" It is a question of power or ability as well as justice.

Confessing His Futility

Then Job goes into considerable detail to spell out his belief that no human being can question the wisdom and power of God (9:2–20). Next Job gives vent to the utter futility of his dilemma as he understands it, "If I justify myself [If I'm right], mine own mouth shall condemn me: if I say, I am perfect (innocent), it shall also prove me perverse [my words may betray me]" (9:20).

And so in desperation Job at this point concludes that human beings lack the power to strive with God and the wisdom to argue with Him. In addition God seems too distant to Job—He exerts His power without discrimination on those who are struggling to do the right thing as well as those with evil intent (9:22). Most certainly, through Job's words here we see an innocent, yet questioning man, confessing his feelings of utter futility and hopelessness.

Praying for a Mediator

In the rhetorical style of the ancient East, Job continues to argue his case as he struggles to make sense of his dilemma (9:23–32). We see in these words how Job is longing for God and yet is fearful of Him as he searches for a hope that seems at the moment to elude him. Finally, in desperation he gets an insight far beyond his time as he prays, "Neither is there any daysman betwixt us [no one to arbitrate], that might lay his hand upon us both [no one to judge us]" (9:33).

In these last few verses of Chapter 9 Job seems to be penetrating the future as he probes the idea of God becoming man as a means of closing the dreadful gap between the eternal God and His creation. Without knowing the full meaning of his words, Job is looking ahead to the coming of Jesus Christ, the

God-man Mediator who once and for all closed all gaps between God and people.

From our vantage point in history almost two thousand years after the birth, life, death, and resurrection of Jesus we find it difficult to put ourselves in Job's sandals. Yet, in spite of the fact that we are favored with the history of God at work with His people the Israelites and with the birth of the church, and how God has turned the course of history upside down through the faithfulness of Christians, we, too, at times get distracted by the reality of "unjust" suffering. In our efforts to comprehend how bad things can happen to good people and how bad people seem to escape the consequences of their actions, we encounter Job's dilemma. Yet, we have so much more going for us than Job did as we seek to penetrate the mysteries of our pilgrimage of faith.

Now, out of the depths of his despair Job talks frankly to God and tells Him he is tired of living (10:1). In fact, he lays down the gauntlet with some pretty straight language as he asks God to tell him the reason God is treating him so badly—". . . shew me wherefore thou contendest with me" (10:2). Job's boldness in talking as he does to God indicates beyond doubt that he wasn't harboring secret feelings of guilt. He has to be innocent of any wrong, otherwise he wouldn't have dared to say such things as, "Is it good unto thee that thou shouldst oppress [Does it make You happy to oppress me]?" (10:3) . . . "Hast thou eyes of flesh [Do you see the way we do]?" (10:4) . . . "Are thy days as the days of man [Is Your life short like mine]?" (10:5).

Then as Job moves toward the end of his speech, he takes another bold step in his questioning of God as he lists what appear to him to be contradictions in God's behavior. For better understanding I'll paraphrase these questions, "Would You destroy me—Your own creation?" (10:8) . . . "Will You turn me back into dust?" (10:9) . . . "Would You take away the life You gave me?" (10:12) . . . "Why did You allow me to be born?" (10:18).

With that last question, Job's thinking has made a full circle, and he is right back where he started—

Risking God's Wrath

cursing the day he was born. But this time he is not shouting the question to the winds, but to God.

Zophar Personalizes the Attack (11:1–20)
Setting Up a Straw Man

Now, Job's third friend enters the fray, Zophar the Naamathite. We don't know the location of Naamath, for this is the only time this name appears in the Bible. It may have been located east of Arabia, however, we cannot be certain. Speaking last as he does tells us that Zophar was the youngest of the three friends. He doesn't enjoy the confidence of age and experience that Eliphaz had or the security of leaning on tradition as Bildad was comfortable with. Consequently, he now moves in and attacks Job personally by accusing him of glibness, deceit, and even lying. Zophar labels Job's words as a farce that must be answered (11:1–3).

Zophar was then guilty of a further exhibition of his own lack of maturity by personalizing his attack and making the mistake of putting words into Job's mouth, "For thou hast said, My doctrine is pure [what I believe is without error], and I am clean [pure, spotless] in thine [God's] eyes" (11:4). Although in his agony Job had made some rash statements, he had never been guilty of such presumptuous and arrogant claims. Over and over again Job had admitted that he wasn't equal to God's wisdom and he had confessed his sinfulness.

The Sound of Fanaticism

From the very beginning of his remarks Zophar seems to have displayed contempt for Job. Instead of being a comforting friend his comments have all the earmarks of any self-righteous enemy on the attack. Most certainly, who needs enemies when a person has a friend like Zophar! This truth is underlined as Zophar next presumes to know what God would say if He spoke to Job (11:5–6).

These words of Zophar's classify him as a religious fanatic—a person who speaks as God would if He had all the facts. After all, with Zophar on the scene God doesn't have to say a word, Zophar speaks for Him! Imagine the unmitigated gall of such a claim. And yet how often we run into folks who claim to know exactly what God wants and who claim to speak for Him. I've run into people, as I'm sure you have, who act as if they had all of God's answers.

But Zophar isn't through, for we now see him move in for the kill as he labels Job a witless donkey who lacks understanding (11:12). And then, having driven home the ultimate insult, Zophar moves quickly now with the pompous assurance that in spite of all this, if Job will just repent of his wickedness God will restore his health and prosperity (11:13–20).

Job Defends His Intellect (12:1–14:22)

All of the ground rules for argument and debate have now changed. No longer does the discussion center on Job's irrational outburst—his intellect is now in question. Is he a wise man or a witless donkey? So often a confrontation like this begins with an objective issue and ends in a personal attack. Whether in a formal debate over a nuclear army or a family discussion over money, the turning point comes when one party accuses the other by saying, "You said. . . ."

The Jagged Edge of Sarcasm

But as we've already learned, Job is a fighter. The trigger edge of sarcasm is felt in his quick response, "No doubt but ye are the people, and wisdom shall die with you. But I have understanding [good sense] as well as you; I am not inferior to you: yea, who knoweth not [doesn't know] such things as these? (12:2–3).

At the same time Job admits that he has been severely stung by the attack of his friends. Furthermore, by their words and attitude, Job says they have made him a mere laughingstock even though he is innocent (12:4). Indeed, none of us can stand being laughed at. A comic once said that if his audiences begin to laugh *at* him rather than *with* him, he'll know that his act is over. Job is saying the same thing. If they take him seriously, he still has hope; if they laugh at him, all hope is gone. Ridicule is the ultimate insult and the cruel destroyer of hope.

Images of Overkill

Job responds to their ridicule with sarcasm, as he pokes his own fun at his friends who have called him a witless donkey and have acted as if he knows nothing about the wisdom and power of God. With delicious humor he suggests that they could learn a great deal about the realities of life by consulting with animals and birds and even fish (12:7–8). Then, with eloquent overkill, Job cites example after example of God's all-knowing and all-powerful ways (12:17–25). And as Job moves toward the end of this part of his response, he shows how deeply they have hurt him by saying again, "What ye know, the same do I know also: I am not inferior unto you [I am as good as you are]" (13:2).

Taking a Chance on God

Job's friends have let him down in his hour of need. They have misunderstood him and lied about him. Now he urges them to keep still while he takes his case to God (13:3–14). Then come those frequently quoted words, "Though he slay me, yet will I trust in him" (13:15).

Even though Job is suffering and being terribly misunderstood by his friends, his relationship with God remains secure. Over the years he has learned that God is absolutely reliable—He can be counted on! As I look at the small risks that I have taken in trying to do the will of God, I have counted on His promises for me and my family, and never once has He failed me. In fact, God has always done more than I expected.

Next, we see in our Scripture lesson that Job turns from his friends who have failed him and takes his case directly to God (13:18). But in doing this he makes two requests, "Withdraw thine hand far from me [remove Your hand from me]: and let not thy dread make me afraid [take away my fear of You]" (13:21).

This is an amazing case of pure grit—if God will grant these two requests, Job is willing to take his chances and demand from God a hearing about his sins. He is making himself completely vulnerable as he insists that either God has to show him his hidden sin or give him an explanation for his suffering (13:22–28). Is it arrogance or trust that makes Job so bold? To us, he appears arrogant, but before passing judgment we must remember the desperation of his suffering and the trust that won't be shaken even though God slays him.

Now as Job continues to lay his case and arguments before God in an effort to understand why all of this is happening to him, he questions God as to the ultimate meaning of life after all (14:1–6). We catch a hint of pessimism as he speaks of the shortness and hardship of human life. And then Job refers to the hopelessness of human death, which is unlike a tree that when cut down can sprout again, "But man dieth, and wasteth away: yea, man giveth up the ghost, and where is he?" (14:10).

Grasping at Straws of Faith

In these words, Job is obviously struggling with the idea of death without the hope of eternal life—the prevailing view that people held at that time. In this desperate struggle with pain and loss everything Job believes and knows about God is being tested. The conflict is just as wrenching as the dilemma of his suffering without having sinned. Yet, because he dares to ask the question, out of his despair comes the far-sighted glimpse of a future hope, "If a man die, shall he live again? . . . will I wait, till my change come" (14:14).

Hope against Hope

Yet, throughout these closing verses of our Scripture lesson (14:15–22) we have a picture of a lonely man caught in the despair of his present pain as he wrestles with his own question, "What is man?" In this picture we see him moving from glimmers of faith to the seeming utter futility of his circumstances. But throughout his struggle we also see a man who refuses to give up his trust in God as he grasps for the straws of a living faith out of which he can rebuild a lasting hope.

Who of us in the hard times and desperate struggles of life in the confusing world of the late-twentieth century cannot identify with this ancient man who was trying to make sense out of his life somewhere in the eastern desert? Our struggles for identity and meaning in a fast changing culture can be devastating. We live under the threat of nuclear war in a space-age world, and we're anxious about traveling in parts of the world for fear of terrorist attacks on our plane or ship. Just beneath the surface of the ordinary routine of our everyday existence, there's a certain madness that can so easily shake the foundations of our lives—a madness that drives many into drug and alcohol abuse as means of escape.

But there is no need for the Christian to plunge into despair and lose hope—either in this life or in anticipation of the next. Paul, the great first-century apostle, in writing to the beleaguered Christians at Corinth, said it well, "We are troubled on every side, yet not distressed; we are perplexed, but not in despair; Persecuted, but not forsaken; cast down, but not destroyed; Always bearing about in the body the dying of the Lord Jesus [Jesus' death], that the life also of Jesus might be made manifest in our body" (2 Cor. 4:8–11).

And Peter gave us this marvelous statement about our hope when he wrote, "Blessed be the God and Father of our Lord Jesus Christ, which according to his abundant mercy hath begotten us again unto a lively [living] hope by the resurrection of Jesus Christ from the dead" (1 Peter 1:3).

Matthew Henry, noble Christian of a past generation and commentary writer, expressed it well when he wrote, "The ground of our hope is Christ in the world, but the evidence of our hope is Christ in the heart"—and with Christ in our hearts we can handle anything that happens.

Lord Jesus, Thank You for the hope You've given me. AMEN.

WHAT THIS SCRIPTURE MEANS TO ME
Job 4:1—14:22

He was too young to die. He had only meant to go to bed that night, but instead he had died, quickly and without apparent reason. He had simply, in a moment, died.

The stunned, pale faces of his children looked up at me, and I, dry-mouthed and tear-filled, was helpless before their agony. My friends, his beautiful widow, who only moments before had gloried in being his wife, sat mute, receiving condolences all through the night. Life's harsh knife had severed this family; death had ravaged the security and contentment of a happy unit.

Spring's dawn mocked us as we made our way home the next morning. I shuddered in the warm morning, clutching my family to me, as if by my own efforts I could keep them alive. I wanted to run away from my thoughts, thoughts that nauseated me with the closeness and quickness of death's striking. If tragedy could strike in that family, what was to keep it from storming down the doors of my house!

The horror of that night sweeps over me still, and then is followed by a wave of sorrow that nothing I could say could put things back together. Nothing I could do could change the unthinkable. I had stood helpless before the anguish of a reluctant widow and her fatherless children.

And so, it seemed, I bumbled my way through that first year of her grief, often doing and saying just the wrong thing, all the time wanting to do the right thing. Indeed, it seemed at times that if my approach wasn't working, I would just do more of it.

Often, I was aware that my feeble attempts to "help" were more for my benefit than for my friend. Uncomfortable in the presence of her grief, I worked hard to make myself feel better. Unable to do anything about her situation, I resorted to words that seemed empty and shallow and trite.

It is one thing to understand the well-known process of grief and to intellectualize about which stage someone is in. It is something else again to experience that process in the everydayness of putting life back together.

It is pretty easy to stand back from a situation and give advice on how to handle the suffering. Dancing on the razor edge of raw grief while trying to carry on with some semblance of normalcy is a different kind of challenge. Analyzing is safe; living through the valley of the shadow of death does indeed thrust one to the outer limits of human understanding.

It is much easier, in the face of another's suffering, to offer advice and counsel than it is to understand the depth of the pain. Telling a hurting person what he should or should not have done is much safer than getting up under that friend's burden and helping him carry it. It is far easier to hide in sermonizing and in sweet platitudes than it is to get mixed up with the messiness of grief.

Lecturing, blaming, and making judgments keep me at a safe distance from the pain. After all, if I can assume a position of authority and show that I *know* better, perhaps I will also show that I deserve to avoid that particular cross.

With months behind us, now I know that what my friend really needed was not answers nor solutions, but my presence, and that my silences were probably more helpful than my words.

With the reality of loss becoming clearer each week, my friend is touching the grace that comes in the midst of the storm. With her faith bought with a price more precious than gold, she lives the words, "Though he slay me, yet will I trust in him."

And I? She has forgiven me for not comforting her perfectly, and so I, too, have touched that grace.

LESSON 4
JOB 15:1–21:34

The Test of Conduct

Lord, Let my conduct, my demeanor, my actions, and my attitudes reflect Your love and power in the world. AMEN.

Disputes in the ancient Wisdom School of the Middle East went in cycles. After each speaker, from the eldest to the youngest, had his turn and the object of the discussion had responded, the cycle was repeated. Now, in this second cycle both the tone and target changes.

Eliphaz illuminates the change of tone in his opening statement. In his words we see nothing of his earlier moderate attitude as he lashes out at Job and labels him a fool with empty notions (15:2a), a bag of hot air from the "east wind" off the desert (15:2b), and a sinner condemned by a crafty (deceitful) tongue (15:5).

In twentieth-century language Eliphaz then goes on to ask, "Who do you think you are?" With heartless tones he drives his point home as he asks, "Art thou the first man that was born? or wast thou made before the hills?" (15:7) and "What knowest thou, that we know not? what understandest thou, which is not in us?" (15:9). Eliphaz is convinced that Job's

Eliphaz Delivers His Second Speech (15:1–35)
An Angry Statesman

trouble was brought on by sin, and he is outraged at Job's insistence that he is innocent. Job's attitude goes against everything Eliphaz believes. It is this that outrages Eliphaz, wise man that he is. This is why he now asserts, "I will shew [show] thee, hear me; and that which I have seen I will declare; Which wise men have told from their fathers, and have not hid it" (15:17–18). With these words Eliphaz boasts of his superior wisdom which is his both through personal visions and traditions of the wise men, past and present.

Profile of Suffering

It is plain to see that Eliphaz sees himself as one of the wisest of men, and as such, Job has no choice but to hear him out and follow his advice. From our perspective Eliphaz seems to be pulling rank on Job. There's an arrogance in Eliphaz's attitude and words that seems familiar as we remember certain people who *are always right,* who always have an answer— especially for *your* problem. It seems there's one in every crowd who is ready to point the finger and declare boldly, "He brought it on himself!"

But although his tone softens a bit Eliphaz now spells out in unvarnished language the kind of suffering a wicked and sinful person goes through: torment (15:20), terror (15:21), despair (15:22), distress (15:24), anguish (15:24), and defiance (15:26). His point is clear. These are all things Job is experiencing—so he must be guilty.

Punishment of the Wicked

Then, having given a step-by-step description of how a sinful person will suffer because of his action, Eliphaz launches into a tirade describing the punishment for someone who has sinned grievously: "He dwelleth in desolate [ruined, deserted] cities" (15:28); "He shall not be rich" (15:29); "He shall not depart out of darkness [escape darkness]" (15:30); there's no payoff in trusting something that is useless (15:31). Then, with colorful picture language Eliphaz concludes his description of punishment by saying that the sinful person will be utterly useless and non-productive before his time (15:32–33).

A Chasm Is Created

Throughout his speech-attack Eliphaz hasn't once mentioned Job by name, but his very words have created a chasm between himself and his old friend. It hadn't been too long ago that he considered Job a wise and honored friend. It was friendship that had driven Eliphaz over the long miles to see his friend. But now Job is seen as hopelessly irredeemable, a man who liked the company of godless people, who profited from bribery, and who was deceitful (15:34–35).

Consistency and vulnerability are extremely important in all of our relationships. Judgmental attitudes cut deep when people are going through difficult times. It is then that they need us to be *with* them, supporting and loving them, not attempting to establish cause. I've known people of influence and leadership who under normal circumstances were gentle and understanding, but when they thought they were being questioned or threatened, they became vicious, defensive, and judgmental. This is precisely what is happening in the Job story at this point.

Bedouin tents have not changed much, if at all, from the time of Job to the present day. It would have been in a setting something like this that Job and his friends carried on their heated discussions.

Job Longs for a Mediator
(16:1–17:16)
*An Appeal for
Understanding*

As Job begins his response to Eliphaz this time, we pick up the tone of a weary and disconsolate man who speaks of his friends as "miserable comforters" who substitute long-winded speeches for a caring attitude (16:2). Then he pictures a reversed situation where they are suffering. He says if that were the case he could talk the way they have, "I could heap up words against you, and shake mine head at you" (16:3–4). To shake or wag one's head was a sign of being happy over someone else's misfortune. But then he heaps coals of fire on them by suggesting that if they were in trouble, he wouldn't do any of those things. Instead, he would speak comforting words of encouragement that would help them in their time of grief and pain (16:5).

The implication is clear as Job continues to appeal for understanding from his friends—if they were to walk in his sandals for awhile, they might feel differently! Then he turns to God and admits that he is desolate and intensely weary and that he feels God has turned against him (16:7–9).

But that isn't all. Not only does Job feel alienated from God, but his friends and neighbors have turned against him. In Job's words we hear intense feelings of alienation and aloneness. Everyone has turned against him; he is alone. Nobody cares. He is nobody. And as Mother Teresa of Calcutta has said, "One of the greatest diseases is to be nobody to anyone."

Then out of the depths of his despair Job likens God to an angry animal that grips his prey in his teeth and shakes them (16:9–12). He then continues and pictures God as an archer who uses him as a target (16:12–13) and as a warrior who lunges at him in combat (16:14). It is easy to see from this picture language Job's deep feelings of hurt over what he believes to be God's actions toward him. Yet Job insists that his integrity is untarnished, he is innocent of any wrong directed either toward God or his fellowman (16:17).

If Only I Had a Mediator

Out of the depths of this moment of despair a profound spiritual insight flashes into Job's thinking and then into his words as he envisions a time when Someone whom he identifies as "my witness . . . in heaven, and my record [advocate] . . ." will intercede for him (16:19–21). Certainly Job could not be aware of the full implications found in this flash of insight. But we see in this a foreshadowing of things to come many centuries later when the "Witness," the "Advocate," the "Intercessor" would be none other than Jesus Christ.

Paul captured this eternal truth in his letter to the Christians in Rome when he wrote, "Who is he that condemneth? It is Christ that died, yea rather, that is risen again, *who is even at the right hand of God, who also maketh intercession for us"* (Rom. 8:34, italics mine).

We will do well to listen closely when desperate people speak. Their cries of anguish need to be heard with understanding, and their flashes of insight should be treated as gems of the Spirit. During his times of prosperity Job didn't see any need for an Intercessor. But after losing everything and teetering on the edge of death under what was thought to be an attack from God, he realized his need of a Savior and Advocate.

This eternal truth has remained unchanged with the passing of centuries. As Christians we grow as we struggle through difficult and perplexing moments. The ease of success—times when everything is running smoothly and without a hitch—seem somehow to inhibit our growth as persons. So often it is in our hard times, our periods of adversity, that we experience those new moments which lead toward maturity. I have a writer friend who hesitatingly admits that some of his best writing has come out of the intensity of personal struggle and difficulty.

Refusing to Budge

But as Job continues his response to his friends, we see his high moment of insight followed immediately by despair as he slumps back once again to await his journey to a place of no return (16:22). After all, the thought of a Witness or Mediator in heaven is absurd when there is no hope of eternal life. A depressive hopelessness descends on him again as with a broken spirit he settles back to wait for his death.

He is terribly alone. His friends are no help. He

sees them as "mockers" whose eyes are filled with hostility (17:2). And he sees himself as the object of bitter misunderstanding (17:4) and denunciation (17:6). Yet, somehow, a ray of hope causes him to dig in his heels and say, "The righteous also shall hold on his way [a righteous person will hold steady], and he that hath clean hands shall be stronger and stronger" (17:9). In spite of the dark cloud of adversity and depression that hovered over him, I wonder if at this point there wasn't a hint of what the writer of the Book of James had to say centuries later, "The effectual fervent prayer of a righteous man availeth much" (James 5:16b).

Job Taunts His Accusers

As Job moves now toward the close of his argument at this point, he seems to be taunting his friends. It is true he feels intense despair because it seems God is afflicting him with almost more than he can handle. But he has held steady in spite of the attacks of his friends and their misunderstandings. Now he seems to be suggesting that they try again (17:10). They've accused him falsely based on their distorted idea of wisdom. With one last jab Job scoffs at their glib promises of hope. Their false interpretation of his trouble has turned his day into the blackness of night, and yet out of that darkness there is the suggestion the light is near at hand (17:12).

Job's understandable sarcasm in this part of his response is superb. And he now closes his speech by daring his friends to answer the question, "And where is now my hope? as for my hope, who shall see it?" (17:15). He seems to be saying that if he is without hope and dies, the same fate will be theirs, and they will all end up in the grave (17:16).

Bildad Replies to Job (18:1–21)

As Bildad responds to Job's anger and sarcasm, he adds fuel to the disagreement as he accuses Job of treating them like dumb animals (18:3). He seems to forget that Zophar started the name-calling when he referred to Job as a witless donkey (11:12). Name-calling always hurts. The childhood ditty about sticks and stones hurting but name-calling being harmless is a myth. Angry and false words wound deeply, and to attach labels to people simply because they don't see things our way goes against the high mark that Jesus set for us.

The differences between Job and his friends have come into sharp focus through the heat of their discussion. To Bildad and his two colleagues the idea or doctrine of "natural justice" must be defended. The payoff for sin was natural disaster. This simply meant that if a person was sick or suffered loss through the forces of nature, that person must have sinned and was being punished. Consequently, Bildad and the others rejected Job's inference that his suffering was an exception that required the setting aside of nature's laws (18:4).

So, with all of this in mind Bildad now proceeds to give us a profile of a person who is sinful and wicked (18:5–21). Nowhere in this profile does Bildad mention Job by name, but his wording is so specific that it is obvious that from his viewpoint he is describing Job.

Bildad Defends His Idea of God's Justice

To fortify the defense of his beliefs Bildad now proceeds to spell out in clear and simple language all of Job's losses—

The Listing of Job's Losses

- the loss of visibility (18:5–6)
- the loss of vigor (18:7)
- the loss of freedom (18:10)
- the loss of peace (18:11)
- the loss of health (18:13)
- the loss of security (18:14)
- the loss of name (18:17)
- the loss of belonging (18:18)
- the loss of children (18:19)
- the loss of fame (18:20)

As Bildad has carefully cataloged all that Job has lost and suffered, for him, the conclusion is clear. Blind to any other alternatives, Bildad now makes it clear that anyone who suffers such losses is not only guilty of wicked behavior but is sinful at the very core of his being and "knoweth not God" (18:21). Bildad and his friends were so steeped in the dogma of their time that there was just no other answer.

I'm always fearful of people who make a practice of posting sin lists, for behind their particular list is a prejudice they want to prove. Then I'm even more fearful of those whose list is impersonal and full of generalities because underneath it all somewhere there is a person or a cause they are attacking. And I am deathly fearful of those who attach a list of sins to people that are suffering and going through hard times. Behind their "good intentions" is a desire to destroy.

Job Anticipates Jesus Christ (19:1–29)

True to the nature of suffering, Job's emotions continue in a roller coaster pattern. Now, rather than answer Bildad's not too thinly veiled accusation in anger, Job appeals to his friends one more time, "How long will ye vex [torment] my soul, and break me in pieces with words?" (19:2). His torment comes from their refusal to accept his innocence and suffering. So, he now insists that if he has sinned, the responsibility is his and not theirs—it is between him and God alone. They should stop playing God. Judgment belongs to Him, not to them (19:5–6).

On the Brink of Blasphemy

Then, as if overwhelmed by all that has happened, Job's words now border on blasphemy as he seems to shout that he has been wrong in his understanding of things and there is no justice (19:7). God has remained silent and has deserted him. God doesn't hear his cries for help; he is fenced in and can't see for the darkness; his identity is gone and everything has been uprooted and is in shambles; and God's wrath has descended on him full force (19:6–12). Then as if to back up everything he feels, Job proceeds to catalog his own list of losses.

The Losses That Count

Job's list includes some of what has already been mentioned along with some that haven't been mentioned before. As Job sees it, he has been—

- alienated from brothers (19:13)
- estranged from acquaintances (19:13)
- deserted by kinfolk (19:14)
- a stranger to those who had been guests in his home (19:15)

- unanswered by servants (19:16)
- an offense to his wife (19:17)
- repulsive to brethren (19:17)
- scorned by little children (19:18)
- detested by his most intimate friends (19:19)
- rejected by loved ones (19:19)

With the completion of this list we have been exposed to the raw edges of Job's suffering. For the most part, Bildad's list didn't focus on the deepest hurts. But as we examine Job's list we see that his greatest loss is not fame or fortune, but friends and family. And while his physical suffering is brutal, it is the loss of human relationships, loved ones and friends, that has reduced him to skin and bones (19:20).

Every student of psychology is introduced to the term "marasmus," to waste away from lack of love. In a classical study of newborn babies who were placed in orphanages, one group received no human touch other than necessary care for feeding and changing. Another group experienced touching and talking, holding and cuddling, from nurses and attendants.

It wasn't long until a marked difference could be seen in the two groups. Those who received no indication of human love began to show severe symptoms of physical illness, mental retardation, and emotional stunting. Only the intervention of human care saved them from death. The other newborns, however, developed as healthy babies even though they were in an orphanage. The marasmus group who were wasting away from lack of love best described Job's deepest suffering, "All my inward friends abhorred me: and they whom I loved are turned against me. My bone cleaveth to my skin and to my flesh [I'm only skin and bones], and I am escaped with the skin of my teeth" (19:19–20).

Job has hit bottom. Despite his further frantic appeal to his friends for pity, he remains alone with the God he believes has struck him down (19:21–22).

The Stubbornness of Job

Much has been written about the "patience" of Job in suffering. He was also stubborn. After accusing

77

God of attacking him wrongly, one would think that he would give up on God. But not stubborn Job. Still holding on to his innocence, he wishes that his protest could be "printed in a book!" or "graven with an iron pen and lead in the rock for ever!" (19:23–24).

Evidently, Job has given up any hope that his innocence will be proven in his lifetime. Only history could judge him. So, he puts his last shred of hope in a permanent record for future generations to read.

The Value of a Good Name

A "good name" meant everything in Job's society. Even though he had lost his sons and his money through catastrophe, he still wanted to keep his reputation as a man of integrity. Sometimes this drive for a place in history backfires. Presidents of major corporations and of the United States can be obsessed by this drive. The last four presidents of the United States, with one eye cocked toward their place in history, have made decisions that put a shadow over their presidencies. Although time has a way of balancing out these decisions with recognition of their contributions, the shadow of doubt can linger on for many years.

Job's reputation was shadowed only by unexplained suffering. His erstwhile friends condemned him as a sinner and God had not moved to restore him. Job knew that if he died, the shadow would remain. So, stubborn in his innocence and adamant about his reputation, he prayed for a written record and an engraved rock that would not only outlive him, but also the religious idea that labeled him a sinner.

The Ultimate Trust

Immediately following that prayer, the curtain of revelation rises and Job clutches at one of the most amazing truths that undoubtedly staggered his imagination. Without knowing the full implications of his words Job said, "For I know that my redeemer liveth, and that he shall stand at the latter day upon the earth: And though after my skin worms destroy this body, yet in my flesh shall I see God" (19:25–26).

It's Handel's *Messiah* thousands of years in advance. Our imagination shows Job standing on his ash heap, tall before God, his eyes seeing through to the centuries to the coming of Christ, and his face aglow with the presence of God.

We stand on the pinnacle of truth in the Old Testament. No book of the Bible or passage of Scripture is more profound than this revelation of God to Job. Think of it. In the capsule of one brief sentence, Job anticipates Jesus Christ, His Incarnation, His Atonement, and His Resurrection.

The Pinnacle of Truth

What more can we say about our faith than to declare, "I know that my Redeemer liveth." Job is so far ahead of his time that only the Holy Spirit could have led him to this affirmation of faith.

A Living Redeemer

But what a contrast! After giving up on his friends, accusing God of wronging him, and admitting that he has no hope left in this life, the Spirit of God lifts him to the highest heaven and gives him a personal glimpse of his Living Redeemer. Earlier, Job prayed in vain for a Mediator and Witness who would stand between him and God to plead his case. Now, God answered his prayer, but with a Redeemer who is far more than a Mediator.

Redemption is a term that comes from the image of the marketplace where a precious item is bought back by its original owner. The story is told about a boy who spent many hours building a model sailboat. On its maiden voyage on the lake, a brisk breeze whisked it out of sight and on to parts unknown. The boy grieved over the loss of his creation until one day he passed a shop window in a neighboring town. Centered in the window was his sailboat with a price tag. Hurrying into the shop, the boy told the owner that the boat belonged to him, but without proof the owner insisted on his price. For weeks the boy worked until he earned enough to buy back his boat. As he held it in his hands once again, he said, "You're twice mine now because first I made you, and now I've bought you back."

Redemption is God's double payment for us. First, He made us for Himself and when sin took us away from Him, He bought us back at the cost of His Son, Jesus Christ. Only love can redeem. So, God assures

Understanding the Atonement

Job of far more than the vindication of his innocence sometime in the future. He lets him know that he is loved, not because he is innocent, but because he is God's creation and needs to be redeemed. In Job, we see our hope. Whatever our physical, emotional, social, or spiritual condition may be, the eternal assurance is ours. We are twice God's. He made us and, through Christ, He bought us back.

Anticipating the Incarnation

Once Job caught the vision of a living Redeemer, his faith took wings. Far, far ahead of his time, he anticipated the incarnation of Jesus Christ as his living redeemer as he proclaimed, ". . . he shall stand at the latter day upon the earth" (19:25).

Through the rising curtain of God's revelation, Job seemed to catch a glimpse of what the Apostle John would write about many centuries in the future, "And the Word was made flesh, and dwelt among us, (and we beheld his glory, the glory as of the only begotten of the Father,) full of grace and truth" (John 1:14).

No idea of God could be more radical for Job's world. To the common people, God was thunderous power; to the scholars of the Wisdom School, He was unswerving justice. At best, Job's vision was fantasy; at worst, it was heresy. A distant God would never stand upon the earth, much less stoop to save sinful humanity. Either great faith or utter foolishness prompted Job's vision. Today, no doubt remains— Job stood on a pinnacle of Old Testament faith and anticipated the future when God became man in Jesus Christ.

You can test true and false prophets from this experience of Job. True prophets see and speak truth which is a natural extension of their own spiritual experience. As we review the life of any biblical prophet—Isaiah, Jeremiah, Daniel, Jonah, or John the Baptist—we see behind their prophetic pronouncements encounters with God, which prepared them as cleansed and disciplined instruments through whom God could speak. False prophets, however, engage in wild leaps into the future apart from their own spiritual history. Their so-called prophecies are disconnected from their character and usually serve their own purposes.

We do well today to beware of this kind of false prophet. As our world becomes more computerized, we feel as if we are losing control of our destiny. When this happens, we turn to prophetic types who seem to see the future or have a word from the past. Christian people are often duped by such spiritual pretenders. But the word of God warns us to "try [test] the spirits [to see] whether they are of God" (1 John 4:1).

Seeing even farther into the future, Job bursts all of the bounds of the limited revelation of his time to envision the resurrection of his body from death. This is his greatest leap of faith. According to natural revelation, death meant the end to human existence. Only an unknown land of shadows awaited him. It would take a giant step of faith to believe and declare that there was life after death. Yet, Job's faith literally launched him into an orbit beyond human imagination when he said, "And though after my skin worms destroy this body, yet in my flesh shall I see God: Whom I shall see for myself, and mine eyes shall behold, and not another" (19:26–27).

Anticipating the Resurrection

What confidence! With these words Job joined a select company of people in the Scriptures who said, "This I know." David the Psalmist wrote, "Be still and *know* that I am God" (Psa. 46:10 italics mine). Blind Bartimaeus testified, ". . . one thing I *know,* that, whereas I was blind, now I see" (John 9:25b, italics mine). And, of course, the Apostle Paul wrote, "I *know* whom I have believed . . ." (2 Tim. 1:12, italics mine). None of these declarations, however, required more farsighted faith than Job's. From the depths of his most horrendous suffering, when his human support system was shattered, Job dared to affirm his faith in God. It was then he was apparently able to catch a vision of that time when he would be personally and bodily joined as a redeemed soul with a loving God in eternal life.

As quickly as Job had climbed to the summit of faith, he fell back into the pain of his suffering at the hands of his friends. Turning to them once again, he concludes his response to Bildad with a word of truth out of which the sting of personal sarcasm has been

Reversing the Sword of Judgment

taken. With straightforward language he reminds his friends that if what he has seen is true and they continue to judge and condemn him, they will come under the sword of God's judgment (19:29).

Zophar Preaches in Self-Defense (20:1–29)

We usually hear what we want to hear. Even though Job spoke prophetic truth which is the hope of humankind, Zophar heard it as an insult to his intelligence. By his own description, he is boiling inside because Job has struck him a telling blow. More than Zophar's faith has been questioned; his ego has been threatened.

When we are threatened, we always resort to our favorite defense mechanism. This time Zophar resorted to reason, or what he calls "The spirit of my understanding" (20:3). Whether he knows it or not, he has exposed the weakness of his faith. Reason has become his substitute for dependence upon God. Zophar assumed that logic alone could answer any question or resolve any issue—intellectual, moral, emotional, or spiritual. So, with reason as his weapon, he tried to take the offensive by preaching a sermon that is a model of sound thinking and good style.

An Almost Perfect Sermon

As you would expect, Zophar's near-perfect sermon has three points: 1) the joy of the wicked is temporary (20:4–11); 2) the sin of the wicked is secret (29:12–19); 3) the punishment of the wicked is sure (20:20–29).

Temporary Joy

As Zophar speaks again, he appeals to the wisdom of the ages as the source for his authority, "Knowest thou not this of old, since man was placed upon earth, That the triumphing of the wicked is short, and the joy of the hypocrite [the godless] but for a moment [is short]?" (20:4–5).

To prove the point that the joy of the wicked is temporary, Zophar cites the evidence that the wicked die young (20:7), disappear without a trace (20:7–9), and leave their children to beg from the poor (20:10).

Secret Sin

Zophar then goes on to show that the sin of the wicked is secret (20:12–19). He admits readily that outwardly it appears as if the wicked and godless person is happy and prosperous, but insists that this is only a ruse because deep down he is already experiencing the judgment of God. This is colorfully pictured by the Job writer—what is sweet in the mouth of a godless person is sour in his stomach (20:12–14); what he swallows in riches is vomited up again (20:15); and what he makes in profit from his business gives him no enjoyment (20:18). Then Zophar goes on to explain why this is so: "Because he hath oppressed and hath forsaken the poor: Because he hath violently taken away [appropriated] a house which he builded not [didn't build]" (20:19).

With these words Zophar has made a logical jump that cannot be justified. He is assuming that people get rich by oppressing the poor and stealing from others. Of course, there are many cases where he is right. But to make every rich person an oppressor and a thief is not only false, it is viciously false.

Up to this point, Zophar's remarks could be taken as a general statement about godless and wicked people in general. But now, his intentions are clear. Under the guise of sound reason, he intends to build an airtight case against Job as the epitome of wickedness. By identifying Job with the wicked rich who oppress the poor and steal from others, he hopes to arouse the sympathy of his listeners who are naturally suspicious of the rich. A dirty trick to be sure, but it is one that works more often than not.

Then, with impeccable logic, Zophar proceeds to prove that the punishment of the wicked is sure, "Surely he shall not feel quietness in his belly [experience no relief from his craving], he shall not save of that which he desired [there isn't anything left for him to eat]" (20:20).

Sure Punishment

The rest of Zophar's descriptive remarks about the punishment the godless person experiences reads like a biography of Job's troubles (20:21–29). Although Zophar still doesn't mention Job specifically by name, there is a direct connection between Zophar's list and Job's experiences of suffering.

For the godless and wicked person food has lost its taste . . . misery has replaced success and well-being

. . . there is no escape from God's judgment . . . he lives in fear and terror and darkness . . . everything he has is lost . . . his sin and guilt are exposed. We see in these verses an unmistakable parallel with what has happened to Job and how he feels about it. In all of this, though, we are keenly aware that Zophar has grossly misunderstood his friend Job because he adamantly clings to the beliefs of the Wisdom School and his own preconceived notions.

It is impossible to over-emphasize the importance as Christians to not let our prejudices and our bias close our minds to the needs and concerns of others. The first and great commandment is to love, not to judge or condemn. Love is inclusive, not exclusive. This is something Zophar and his two colleagues failed to understand!

Job's Response to Zophar (21:1–34)

As Job responds to these last remarks of Zophar, we get a clear indication that he has not been overwhelmed; he is far from finished. In fact, as we catch the spirit of his words now we get the sense that the momentum of the discussion has shifted. Job has more of the sound of being in charge as he now challenges his friends to stop mocking him, to be quiet and look him in the eye, and above all to listen carefully to what he has to say (21:1–5). Through the fleeting vision of his living Redeemer he has gained a measure of confidence.

Reason Can Be Faulty

Zophar's arguments relied on reason to prove that wicked and godless people will suffer swift and sure punishment for their sins. But Job's suffering had taught him that reason can be faulty, so he now asks the difficult question, "Wherefore do the wicked live, become old, yea, are mighty in power?" (21:7). That is a penetrating question. Why is it that wicked and ungodly people may live to old age and enjoy a prosperous life?

Zophar has said that the joy of godless people is temporary and God's judgment is swift. But now Job is saying that the facts of life contradict Zophar's beliefs. Job is dealing with facts and not theory or philosophy. He has seen people who didn't pay any attention to God live to old age and enjoy prosperity.

He has seen them watch their children and grand-children grow up. He has seen the godless live without fear and acquire great wealth. From all outward appearances they seemed to have it made even though they ignored God (21:8–16).

Job is wrestling with questions we all ask—why is it that Godly people must endure suffering and why should godless people seem to prosper? Why? Why?

Recently I had a telephone call from a relative who had just been diagnosed as having multiple sclerosis. She is a young and beautiful woman, a devoted wife and mother, an energetic person pursuing a nursing career, a gifted artist, a community worker, and a faithful member of her church. Yet she has a degenerative and incurable disease.

When I talked to her husband, his voice choked with emotion as he said, "It's especially hard at Christmas time. We're still trying to handle it." Job could have used them as a part of his argument, for they hadn't denied God or written Him off. And yet, in the prime of their life they are suffering with the reality of an incurable disease that has dashed all their hopes and changed all their plans.

Job continues to press his point (21:17–20). He calls for Zophar to prove, if he can, the rule that suffering and hard times are the result of sin and that God's judgment is swift and sure.

Job is on the winning side of the discussion now. He knows that Zophar's logic is faulty, so now he unleashes a blockbuster as he says, "Shall [Can] any [man] teach God knowledge? seeing he judgeth those that are high [in heaven]" (21:22). Job's sarcasm is classic as he drives his point home. Since Zophar can't prove that he is right, he has not only presumed to speak for God in what he has said, but he has also attempted to tell God how He should act. In all that Zophar has said he has been playing God.

Little has changed even though countless centuries have passed from Job's day to these closing days of the twentieth century. We're still guilty, as Zophar was, of wanting to take matters into our own hands and tell God how to run His world. With classic

Why Do the Righteous Suffer?

Can Anyone Teach God?

85

arrogance we're still not sure God can handle things without our interference. But the words of the wisdom writer are still the best advice we can get, "Trust in the Lord with all thine heart; and lean not unto thine own understanding" (Prov. 3:5).

Ask Any Traveler

As Job moves now toward the end of his response to Zophar, he takes issue with his friend for using tradition as the basis for his reasoning. Rather than look to the wisdom of the past ages for the answer to the why of suffering, Job suggests that a poll be taken with those who have traveled over the road (21:29). In other words, consult with people who have experienced life in the wider world beyond the land of Uz.

Let's face it, tradition has the seeds of weakness in its strength. Tradition gives us continuity with the past, but at the same time it can become a millstone around our necks. We need the roots of tradition, but we also need the shoots of new experience in our search for truth.

In his closing sentences (21:32–33) Job takes a risky position in opposition to his friends and the orthodoxy of his time—suffering is not the automatic consequence of sin any more than prosperity is the guaranteed right of a righteous person. And he brings down the curtain on his remarks by denouncing his friends' position as empty and false (21:34).

There is a boldness in Job's thinking and words now that foreshadows the boldness of Jesus Christ when with considerable risk He opened up the way to new life that threatened the orthodoxy and the "wisdom" of His day.

Father God, Help me to see others the way You do—with eyes of grace, forgiveness, love, compassion. AMEN.

WHAT THIS SCRIPTURE MEANS TO ME
Job 15:1—21:34

"Tell me about this God you don't believe in," the college professor asked. "I probably don't believe in that God, either."

The gentle tone invited response. The quiet and patient waiting gave permission for the student to lay down his tirade of skepticism and anger. In an atmosphere of acceptance, the self-proclaimed agnostic was able to sort through tangled thoughts and near-blasphemous words.

"What does it take to hear God?"

"How could a good God let this happen?"

"Why doesn't God do something about this?"

"I thought God was supposed to be all-powerful!"

The torrent of words spewed across the professor's desk. Pent-up wonderings out of the dark night of intellectual wanderings burst out of the young man's mouth in machine-gun fashion . . . and the professor sat quietly.

"This isn't the God I learned about in Sunday school!" the young man snarled.

At each stage in the pilgrimage of life, I am able to know God with as much maturity as I have at that time. At each stage along the way my tendency is to freeze God; I want Him to stay put in my perception so that I can manage Him. Out of the blue something challenges the view that I have cherished of who God is and what He does. All of a sudden, I am confronted with something I want to dismiss, but cannot, and so I find myself contending with God, trying to get my footing with Him once again.

It's the unanswerable questions of life that make me rethink who God is. It's those unacceptable challenges that take me to the outer limits of understanding. It is those things I want to change but cannot that pit my will against God's and throw me face to face with His sovereignty. Over and over, my old, limited and limiting view of God has to die so that a fuller, more complete concept of who He is can be born. And that often is done with agony.

When God is not who I have thought He was, I tend to fight with Him. I try to force things to be like I want them to be, and then I expect Him to fit in with my agenda. I rush into God's presence, demanding that He listen to me and fulfill my wishes. It occurs to me only later that it is I who am to listen and fulfill His will!

Most of the time, I make God in my image. I think He must have the same limitations that I have, and so I doubt that He really can do what He needs to do. Or I insist that God is like some other earthly vessel, and fall victim to the trap of expecting some human to be divine and forgetting to let the Divine be who He is.

I hold on to my childhood pictures of God. I sift around in the past, looking for God. I shy away from new expressions of the faith. I hide in tradition or I rebel against all forms of religion, thereby depriving myself of comfort.

And when my faith is tested by unanswerable questions, I lash out in anger. I am scared that maybe this time, God has gone for good. I worry that I have strayed so far that God cannot find me, and I yearn for those childhood days when it was easier to believe. I long to return to that state of childish dependence and escape the demands of a mature faith.

Finally, though, through the tumult of my questions and life's certainties, I hear the whisper of grace. The God-who-is-making-all-things-new says to me, "I am the Lord your God, and I will never leave you nor forsake you," and I pull myself up out of my agony to declare, "I know that my redeemer liveth!"

LESSON 5
JOB 22:1–31:40

The Test of Character

Lord Father, Thank You for building up my character, for conforming me into the likeness of Jesus. AMEN.

Job's insistence that his friends' answers are false puts Eliphaz back on comfortable ground again. He cannot handle Job's anger, but he is a master at debating truth and falsehood. As proof of his mastery, he responds by conceding that Job is an example of personal righteousness—even "wise" (22:2) and blameless (22:3).

Eliphaz—One Last Try (22:1–30)

Conceding a point in a discussion or debate is a tricky tactic. The intention is to disarm the other person in order to strike a mortal blow with a surprise attack. In my early years as a high school debater, I remember preparing my case on a strong point that I could both advance and defend in the heat of argument. Experienced debaters, however, know how to fake and feint until they find out where you are strong and weak. Then, they may concede the point where you are strong and advance the point which you are not prepared to defend.

By conceding that Job is righteous, wise, and blameless, Eliphaz takes the risk of losing his argument in order to strike where he assumes that Job is most vulnerable. Eliphaz's ploy is immediately evident. He works on Job's fears, especially his confession that his nights are filled with terror. Confident in his conclusion, he asks, "Will he reprove thee for fear of thee? will he enter with thee into judgment?" (22:4). In effect Eliphaz is saying, "Is it because you are conscientious in religious practices that God rebukes you and puts you on trial?"

While Eliphaz has started on a conciliatory note, he moves now to strike at one of Job's paralyzing weaknesses—fear, an emotion usually associated with sin and guilt. The wisdom writer caught this idea when he wrote, "The wicked flee when no man pursueth" (Prov. 28:1). Guilt produces fear, and fear keeps us on the run.

In spite of what Eliphaz thought, it wasn't guilt that produced Job's fear, but the results of his suffering and his belief that everything which had happened to him was engineered by God. Nevertheless, Eliphaz held tenaciously to his belief that Job had sinned.

I Know How God Thinks

Drawing on what he believes to be his superior wisdom and insight, Eliphaz confronts Job with what he thinks is the root of Job's fears and terror—Job is guilty of social sins. He has demanded unjust collateral (22:6); he has taken people's clothing as surety (22:6); he refused to give water to the thirsty and withheld food from the hungry (22:7); he refused to supply the needs of widows and he robbed orphans (22:9).

Even though these allegations are without substance, Eliphaz makes his point that it is neglect and disregard for the poor and needy that are terrorizing Job and causing him to feel blinded, trapped, and overwhelmed. Job lives, says Eliphaz, in constant fear of retribution from those whom he has wronged (22:10–11).

Eliphaz can make these charges and allegations without having to prove his point simply because in the court of public opinion guilt will more likely be believed than godliness. This is especially true in the case of wealthy and influential people. We love to dabble in gossip about those who one way or another are better off than we are.

Millions of dollars are made each week on "scandal sheets" that carry sensational headlines and unfounded stories about celebrities. And somehow the more bizarre the story, the more ready we are to believe it. It was this way with Job. As the most famous and influential man in all the East before his downfall, he was fodder for the accusations about cheating and stealing as the means for acquiring his wealth. By linking Job's fears with sins against the poor, the widows, and the fatherless, Eliphaz had public opinion on his side. In a strange and unusual way Eliphaz gives the impression that he understands the mind of God, and he has diagnosed Job's weaknesses and sins.

I Know Who God Is

Then, reassuming his role as the senior wise man in the group, Eliphaz breaks forth into a verse or a hymn which magnifies the greatness of God in heaven and acknowledges that He is all-knowing and all-seeing (22:12–14). And then he goes on to imply that this sovereign God, consistent with His character, will bring swift and sure judgment to the godless who have turned on Him, even though He has blessed them (22:14–18). So, under the guise of praising and exalting God, Eliphaz uses this verse or hymn to defend his interpretation of justice, to condemn Job as a sinner, and to demonstrate his superior knowledge of the mind of God.

The temptation to act as if we have an inside track with God plagues us all. It can lead as it did with Eliphaz to a cataloging of the sins of others as if we have the right to speak for God because of an assumed special relationship.

I Know What God Does

With a fresh flood of arrogance Eliphaz continues to play his role as he now offers a sugar-coated recital of exactly how God will bless Job if he will acknowledge his sins and repent. First Eliphaz promises Job that if he will get right with God—submit himself to Him—he will have peace (22:21). If he will "return to the Almighty," he will be restored (22:23). If he will make certain that his home is free from sin and if he will love God instead of gold, the Almighty will reward him (22:24–26).

But that isn't all. Eliphaz goes on to promise Job that when he prays, his prayers will be answered—he will have the new and honored status of an intercessor and a covenant keeper, "Thou shalt pay thy vows" (22:27). Further, he is promised the role of an encourager (22:28) and a mediator (22:29–30). In other words, Eliphaz is promising Job the return of material, social, and spiritual resources if he will but repent.

Now, as grand and glorious as these promises seem, they are still suspect. Is Eliphaz enhancing his own position and role in all of this or is he really interested in Job's welfare? Is Eliphaz genuinely concerned about Job or is his primary purpose to come off looking good and special himself? Based on all he has said here and in his earlier remarks, it seems most likely that what he is really saying to Job is something like this, "If you repent, you will be restored and *become like me.*" Eliphaz's model of spirituality is a clone of himself.

Authentic saints of God are just the opposite. They brag only about God and insist that He alone is worthy of imitation. On the other hand Eliphaz has set himself up as an example for Job to follow. Through all of this Eliphaz has exposed a spirituality that is, at best, shallow and self-centered. As he sees it, high position and prestige belong to a person whose age, wisdom, and righteousness enable him to speak for God to ordinary sinners like Job and to pray for them. The problem is that while Eliphaz knows a great deal about God, his relationship with Him is impersonal. He knows Him as the God of power and justice but not the personal, caring God of love and mercy. Consequently, the Eliphaz approach to human suffering is cold and rational.

Eliphaz's concept of God as a distant, awesome, far-off, and impersonal deity was quite common to the culture of his time. But the God of Adam and Eve, of Noah, and of the early Patriarchs was a personal God who "talked" and "walked" with people. Yes, He was a God of righteousness and justice. But at the same time He was sensitive to human suffering because He was also a God of love and mercy.

As we move into Job's response to Eliphaz, it becomes readily apparent that Job realizes there's no need to be defensive or reactive. His friend's thinking has remained unchanged except his accusations have shifted from rational to emotional grounds and from personal to social sin. Nothing Job has said seems to have made a difference to Eliphaz, yet he continues to be honest about his thoughts and feelings. As Job speaks now we get another in-depth picture of his relationship to God.

In his remarks Eliphaz has claimed to know how God thinks and to understand His actions. By contrast, Job opens his remarks now by candidly admitting that his complaint is bitter and his mind and heart are full of resentment. He speaks of God's hand as still being heavy against him (23:2). These are the words of a man who is very much alone and hurting badly.

Out of his desperation he utters some of the most plaintive and beautiful phrases in all of the book as he pours out his desire and his thirst to find God. "Oh that I knew where I might find him! that I might come even to his seat [to where He lives]! I would order [state] my cause before him, and fill my mouth with arguments. I would know the words which he would answer me, and understand what he would say to me" (23:3–5).

We learn from these words that Job is still presuming that if he could communicate with God he would win his case—he would be proved right. There's an underlying tone in Job's words that God would listen to him and treat him fairly. In contrast to Eliphaz's pompous pronouncements, Job puts confidence in his friendship with God. And perhaps no words in all of the story better express Job's relationship with God than what comes next. Job says that when he has searched for God in the east—"I go forward"—or in the west—"and backward," he doesn't find or see Him. Then when he searches in the north—"On the left hand"—or in the south—"on the right hand," he doesn't find Him (23:8–9). In spite of that, though, Job then adds, "But he [God] knoweth the way that

Job—A Humble Friend (23:1–24:25)

I Cannot Find God

93

I take [He knows where I am]: when he hath tried [tested] me, I shall come forth as gold" (23:10).

Remember, these confident words are spoken out of intense suffering because of his fear of being abandoned by God. Something more than the power and justice of the God of Eliphaz undergirds Job's faith. Rather, he gains his confidence through the knowledge of God as a Friend who watches over every step, feels every pain, and looks forward to the time when His servant will be vindicated.

The holding power of love never fails to amaze me. A colleague told me about his oldest son who had become one of the lost and burned-out souls on the college campus in the early 1970s. Dropping out of school, doing drugs, and denying God, the young man had left home and disappeared into the drug culture. When his father first confided in me, he said that he hadn't heard from his son for months and had no idea whether he was dead or alive. "We pray for him each night," he said. "But only our love can hold him."

A year after that I saw the family in church, and with them was an emaciated young man carrying three Bibles. The father hurried him over to me and proudly announced, "This is my son." Love *had* held him. Since then I have talked a number of times with frantic parents whose children have rejected and left them. With the image of that young prodigal in my mind, I've said with confidence, "Only love can hold him/her now."

I Don't Know Who He Is

With Job's next words we catch the vivid contrast between his faith and that of Eliphaz. Earlier Eliphaz had made the arrogant claim that he knew who God was (22:12–18). Now Job frankly admits, "But he is in one mind, and who can turn him? and what his soul desireth, even that he doeth" (23:13). In other words, Job is saying that God will do what He wants to do and He won't be deterred. In saying this Job readily admits that he doesn't know who God is except that He is unique, unchangeable, and will do whatever He desires. Then, as he continues (23:14–17), he makes it clear to Eliphaz that it is not really knowing who God is, and not the social sins he's accused of, that is the cause of his fear and terror.

And we react exactly like Job did when we encounter the unknown. Certain movies play on our fears of the unknown. I remember so well my feelings when I saw "Close Encounters of the Third Kind." Weird objects, people and happenings from outer space titillated the audience and filled us with feelings of terror. Possibly such movies serve a good purpose in that by living out the fantasy of our fears, we get some relief from the terror of the unknown that lurks within us.

So, we understand that it wasn't the fear of retribution for his sins against people that made Job fearful, but rather fear of the unknown—of not knowing who God is. Because Eliphaz had claimed to know it all, he had no need for faith. But Job's honest confession made faith in God's good purpose his *only* hope.

I Don't Know What God Does

Job moves on now to refute Eliphaz's glossy promise that God will restore him if he repents as he asks, "Why, seeing times are not hidden from the Almighty, do they that know him not see his days?" (24:1). To paraphrase, Job is saying, "If you know so much, why don't we see God's swift and sure judgment on those who are the most wicked?" The point is that if Eliphaz is right, the more sinful and wicked a person is, the swifter should be God's punishment. But it is clear that things don't necessarily work that way, consequently Job freely admits that he isn't able to interpret God's actions.

Rustlers, Robbers, and Rebels

At this point in his response Job seems to look out at the world he knows and express impatience and frustration with God for the sin and evil that is ever present in society. As he does this, he isolates three kinds of wicked people that seem to be unchecked. First, there are the *rustlers* who violently rob people of their land and herds and reduce them to poverty (24:2–8). These rustlers, like those of the old American West, preyed on those who were less fortunate and unable to protect themselves—the orphans and widows.

Second, there are the *robber barons* who exploit the poor and less fortunate by charging excessive interest on their loans and who take advantage of people who for whatever reason are unable to defend themselves. While this kind usually operate within the law, they are still regarded as evil because of the hardship they create (24:9–12).

Third, there are the *rebels*—murderers, adulterers, and thieves who resist the light of God's natural law and violate other human beings under the cover of darkness (24:13–17). These three kinds of rebels perpetuate evil which penetrates all of human society: murder violates reputation and life, adultery violates the sacredness of marriage and home, and stealing violates the sacredness of property. All of these, Job says, work under the cover of the darkness of evil. Jesus described such people and their condition when He said, "And this is the condemnation, that light is come into the world, and men loved darkness rather than light, because their deeds were evil. For every one that doeth evil hateth the light, neither cometh to the light, lest his deeds should be reproved" (John 3:19–20).

As Job surveys this wicked scene, he most certainly agrees with Eliphaz's reasoning that evil and wicked people should be judged quickly, and he is appalled that God doesn't seem to be doing anything about it (24:18–21). As a matter of fact, it seems that God doesn't differentiate between good people and evil people when He passes out natural blessings. Again the words of Jesus speak to Job's dilemma: "for he [God] maketh his sun to rise on the evil and on the good, and sendeth rain on the just and on the unjust" (Matt. 5:45). In reality Job reasoned that by not meting out swift punishment on evil and ungodly people, God was actually being partial for a time (24:18–24).

On that note, Job issues a challenge to Eliphaz and the others, "And if it be not so now [If what I've said isn't so], who will make me a liar [who can prove me wrong], and make my speech nothing worth [say that my words aren't true]?" (24:25). With this challenge Job brings to a close his third response to Eliphaz.

Bildad: The Answer of Futility (25:1–6)

As Bildad speaks now, it is plain to see from his words and attitude that Job's arguments have struck raw nerves. Bildad opens his response to Job with no effort to respond to Job's question. In his frustration and anger, he ignores that completely. Instead, he gives a beautifully worded description of the God he believes in—a far-off impersonal God of power and peace and authority (25:2–3). He exalts God and then turns on Job, declaring that he is sinful in life, he was depraved at birth, and is no better than a "worm" in the eyes of God (25:4–6). From all of this, it seems clear that Bildad's assessment of Job in particular and people in general is dismal.

In Bildad's final words here we have the question, "What is man?" asked either directly or indirectly for the third time. Eliphaz inferred the question at the very beginning of the discussion when he defined the nature of man as one living in a house of clay "whose foundation is in the dust" and is "crushed before the moth" (4:19). Later on Job asks the question directly (7:17–18). And as both Eliphaz and Job have responded to the question, their response has been drastically different. For Eliphaz, man—humankind—is worthless in God's sight. But for Job, man—humankind—is of sufficient importance to command the attention of God *even if that attention is the test of suffering.*

Bildad's View of Humankind

During the days of campus protest in the early 1970s, I attended a meeting of beleaguered college and university presidents. Just before the evening meal the president of a Jesuit college whose office had been trashed by rioting students that week was asked to give the blessing. He prayed, "Lord, we read that those whom You love, you chasten. If it's all right with You, we could get along with a little less love." I suspect that Job must have felt something like that. He was flattered because God was paying special attention to him, but he would just as soon have had a little less attention.

In this brief attack on Job, Bildad exposed the fact that his view of the human race was pretty low, on the level of a worm. And unwittingly he also pictured God as an uncaring monster. The two views are inseparably linked. What we think about God determines how we look at other people—whether we look through lenses of despair or hope.

Bildad's Worm Mentality

Job's Final Answer
(26:1–31:40)

When Bildad lost his cool, he also lost out in the discussion. There was no need for Job to retaliate. Instead, we see him feeling sorry for his friends because they have failed in their mission. Presumed to be comforters, they haven't helped him (26:2); presumed to be wise, they haven't given him any fresh insight (26:3); presumed to be godly, they have spoken only with defensive bitterness (26:4).

The Quality of Counseling

From time to time each of us becomes a counselor for others. And the quality of our counseling is tested by the same three questions Job raised with his friends: 1) Are we encouraging? 2) Are we insightful? 3) Are we gracious?

These three penetrating questions and our responses to them determine the value not only of our counseling but of our daily communication as well. As Christians who represent Christ in our neighborhoods and towns, it is important that we be able to respond affirmatively to all three.

We all know from practical experience that a conversation with certain people leaves us with the taste of ashes in our mouths. The negative attitude of such folks depresses us. On the other hand, a few words with other people send us back into life with fresh hope and an uplifted attitude as we're reminded that God is in His heaven so everything is all right.

After his long conversations with his three friends, I'm sure that Job learned a valuable lesson. If the time ever comes in the future when he is sought out as a counselor, his words will be encouraging, insightful, and gracious—important marks in the conversation of any Christian.

The Edges of His Ways

It isn't surprising at this stage that Job's response to Bildad takes on a completely different tone. For the first time in these extended conversations he places emphasis on the spiritual and mystical nature of God. Up until now the discussion or debate has centered around knowing and understanding God through His natural creation and through human reason. Now, however, Job reminds himself and his friends that God is the powerful and spiritual Creator. In vivid poetry Job speaks of God as forming the sky and suspending the earth in its place (26:7). With reference to the Genesis creation account he credits his God with the separation of the water, with the dividing of light from darkness, and of giving order and form to all of His creation (26:8–13).

Then after painting a vivid picture of the greatness and magnificence of God as seen in His mighty creation activities, Job now says this is just one side of the coin, one side of the story, for all of "these are parts [the edges] of his ways." Nature doesn't begin to show us all of God, and the vast universe is nothing more than a small reflection of God's majesty, a faint whisper of the awe-filled God (26:14).

We see in these words that somehow Job's perception of God has moved from the natural to the spiritual. Like a blind man groping in the dark, Job is searching for—is reaching out to—the God of grace.

As Job finishes this awesome portrayal of a God who is far off and powerful but also near at hand, he seems to pause as if awaiting a response of some kind from Bildad. But Job is now thinking way beyond the boundaries of anything Bildad can understand. To think of creation out of nothingness or mercy out of love is beyond him. In fact, it is beyond the understanding of all three friends, for all are silent.

Job the Teacher

Stimulated by the silence of his friends, Job continues (27:1). Once more, without the slightest hint of an apology, he reaffirms his integrity, his righteousness, and his innocence before God, even though it appears God has turned against him (26:2–6). Then he warns his friends that they, not he, will be the objects of God's judgment (27:7–10). And he next makes the bold and daring pronouncement that must have taken his listeners entirely by surprise, "I will teach you by the hand [power] of God" (27:11).

Earlier, you will recall, it was Eliphaz who adopted the role of a wise teacher with a superior knowledge of God. Now, Job turns the tables and announces that he is the teacher because he has knowledge of the truth which his friends do not have. And with a tinge of sarcasm he justifies his position by saying that if they had known what he now does, they would not have wasted a lot of time in senseless conversation (27:12).

The Sin of the Wicked

Job now shares his thinking with his friends on two subjects—wickedness and wisdom. After all, they had had a great deal to say about these two. Now it is his turn. His comments on wickedness are pretty much a repetition of what has been said before. He agrees with his friends who have developed a portrait of a wicked person as a rich man who oppresses the poor and widows and then lives in terror for fear of reprisal. And he further agrees that such a person will receive God's judgment in due time (27:13–23).

The Search for Wisdom

In speaking of wisdom now Job proves that he has no peer in his understanding of wisdom (28:1–28). In these verses Job, with rare poetic insight, speaks of the marvelous genius of the human mind that can locate and mine precious metals, level mountains, and build dams. He seems to anticipate the advanced technologies of all future time, and then goes on to say that even people who can do all of those things cannot create, discover, buy, or understand the meaning of authentic wisdom. As brilliant as these achievements have been from the beginning of time, none of them gives us definitions of wisdom, for God alone understands it.

Then follows Job's God-given insight, "Behold, the fear of the Lord, that is wisdom; and to depart from evil is understanding" (28:28). In these words he has reaffirmed the essentials of his faith. Yes, he believes in the justice and mercy of God, and he knows that it is through fear of God alone that wisdom is attained.

Job's insights carry a powerful message for late twentieth-century people; and their truth is just as up-to-date today as it was thousands of years ago, except that the technological wonders we take for granted would have been way beyond Job's imagination. Space travel, communication satellites, laser surgery, organ transplants, solar power—all of these and much more are now a part of our daily routines. It is amazing the insights that God has given us. Yet none of these constitute authentic wisdom—it is still the fear of the Lord accompanied by turning our backs on evil that is the source of wisdom. It is not our genius but our knowledge of God that gives true meaning to life.

Holding to the Essentials

When our faith is severely tested, there is the danger of throwing the baby out with the bathwater—of rejecting what has sustained us in the past but doesn't seem to be working now. Job could readily have rejected his past beliefs which seem to have failed him in his time of testing and suffering. But the maturity of his faith is seen in the fact that he could keep the fundamentals of his earlier faith as the foundation on which to build a new and enlarged faith.

Radicals always have the problem of deciding what to keep and what to throw away from their past. But to turn our backs entirely on the past is to be without a foundation on which to build the future. Unlike the "flower children" of the 1960s who seemed to abandon their past in favor of either taking to the hills or joining the establishment and becoming bloodless conformists, Job held steady to the essentials of his beliefs. Instead of succumbing to disillusionment because of reverses and suffering, he continued to believe in the majesty and mystery of God. He still held to his belief in God's justice and was convinced that the fear of the Lord was the beginning of wisdom.

Having restated his beliefs, Job seems to pause again to give one of his friends the opportunity to respond to what he has said, but there is silence. There was nothing that Eliphaz or Bildad or Zophar could add to the discussion. This meant that Job was free to continue. And he does.

The Glory of the Past

Job has spoken boldly about the essentials that hold his faith together. Now he describes the contradiction that tests his faith. In one of the most moving pictures in human literature he recalls the glory of his past and then vividly describes the shame of his present condition. The ability to speak with such candor about this contradiction indicates that Job had worked through his anger and had regained his perspective.

In the opening of the Book of Job we were introduced to him as a righteous man of health, wealth, family, and fame. Now, in his own words we learn the details of the blessing which God had given him. We can identify with him as he says, "Oh that I were as in months past" (29:2). Then he goes on to spell out the past as he says it was then that "God preserved me" . . . it was then "his candle shined upon my head," and it was then "by his light I walked through darkness" . . . it was then "the secret of God was upon my tabernacle [God blessed my home]" . . . it was then "the Almighty was yet with me" and "my children were about me" . . . it was then "I washed my steps with butter [my pathway was wet with cream or milk]" . . . and it was then "the rock poured me out rivers of oil [the rocks were full of olive oil]" (29:2–6). In other words this was a time when God was with him, when his family was intact, and when he had everything for a comfortable life.

As Job continued to explore his memories of past glory another scene fills his mind (29:7–17). He sees himself going to the city gate, taking his place in the seat of honor, and receiving the accolades of the young and old, princes and nobles alike. He remembers, too, that he didn't have their respect primarily because of his wealth and power but because of his compassion for the poor, his right standing with God, and his sense of justice for the oppressed.

Quite in contrast to Eliphaz's accusation that he oppressed the poor, Job remembers that he was actively involved in rescuing them from those who were taking cruel advantage of them (29:17). In other words, Job saw himself as a man who in the affairs of city life was attentive to the needs of people less fortunate than he was.

Job's honesty is refreshing. Even though in the past he expressed his gratitude for God's blessings, he now realizes that he took them for granted. He admitted that he expected to die in comfort after living out a long life with health, wealth, and glory

(29:18–20). How like Job most of us are! We, too, are guilty of taking God's blessing for granted. And the more blessings we have, the more we want and think we deserve. Then, if for whatever reason we don't have what we think we should, we complain and turn against God.

Another scene moves on to Job's memory-stage (29:21–25). He remembers when people everywhere in his part of the country looked him up and asked him for his wise counsel. With this scene we catch another glimpse into Job's soul. We see that his power and influence didn't come from wealth or position but from the wise words and compassionate spirit that he made available to those in need.

Indeed, through Job's memory-rehearsal we gain a new appreciation for the glory of his past. It was the past of a spiritual man who lived in the presence of God, earned the respect of people because of his integrity and compassion, and was known for his wise counsel. In other words, he was a true friend who deserved his reputation of being the greatest man in all the East.

The Shame of the Present

Now, after basking in the glory of his past, Job turns to the shame of his present condition. No human drama is more gripping. Whether from history, literature, theater, or the news, we are all moved by stories of the rise and fall of persons, institutions, and nations. Gibbon's *The Decline and Fall of the Roman Empire* and Dreiser's novel *An American Tragedy* rank among the best of history and fiction. Neither of these, however, is more powerful than the story of Job's fall from glory to shame. But no human story is more powerful than the plunge of Jesus Christ from the glory of heaven to the shame of the cross.

Paul captured the "emptying" of Jesus in his letter to the church at Philippi when he wrote, "Let this mind be in you, which was also in Christ Jesus: Who, being in the form of God, thought it not robbery to be equal with God: But made himself of no reputation [made himself nothing], and took upon him the form of a servant [slave], and was made in the likeness of men: And being found in fashion as a man, he humbled himself, and became obedient unto death, even the death of the cross" (Phil. 2:5–8).

We've seen in our lessons that Job, too, was emptied of his glory. But there is a significant difference between Jesus and Job. Jesus voluntarily gave up his glory and took on the shame of the cross for our salvation. Job, on the other hand, suffered his shame involuntarily. In fact he believed that God had even become an adversary who attacked him for no discernible reason. Now as we move ahead in our lesson, we are exposed to the raw edges of the extremes of Job's glory and his shame. From the respect of all people, Job became the object of mockery by youthful ruffians (30:1–2) . . . from a position of authority, he became powerless at the hands of fools (30:8) . . . from great fame, Job became the butt of cruel jokes (30:9) . . . from the protective comfort of home, he became the victim of terror (30:15) . . . from the picture of health, Job became a bag of bones (30:17–18) . . . from enjoying the presence of God, he became an abandoned person (30:20) . . . from living under God's protection Job became the target of God's attack (30:21) . . . from being a part of the congregation or assembly of God, Job was reduced to a companion of animals (30:28–29) . . . and from the joy of beautiful and happy music, he became the player of dirges (30:31).

Only someone who has known similar heights of glory and depths of shame can identify with Job's dilemma. He is totally perplexed by the contradiction between his circumstances and the teaching of justice that assured him of prosperity because of his righteousness. And so it is that Job, like Jesus, can identify with all who weep and mourn.

The Oath of Innocence

Let's take a close look at Job's reasoning now. First, he declared his faith in the majesty, justice, and wisdom of God (26:1–28:28). Next, he confessed his fall from glory to shame (29:1–30:31). By all counts now he should confess that his suffering is the result of sin. After all, the orthodoxy of Job's times declared that sin results in suffering and righteousness promises prosperity.

But in the depths of his being Job knows that his

troubles are not the result of his sin. For this reason he makes a bold move. He will exercise a special privilege of a person accused of crime before an ancient Eastern court of law—he will take a Public Oath of Innocence. He is willing to write the accusations against him on a placard which he will wear around his neck as he walks through the streets. Everyone he meets will have an opportunity to read the accusations and be a witness against him. It's a big risk, but Job is willing to take it in order to prove his innocence.

I wonder how many of us would be willing to take an Oath of Innocence and wear the list of accusations against us as we walk along the streets. It is more than likely that if we were persons of wealth, power, and fame we would have enemies somewhere who would be more than willing to speak against us. Yet Job takes his chance.

Job's boldness reminds us of Jesus again. As His enemies closed in on Him, He issued the challenge, "Which of you convicts me of sin?" That was His public oath of innocence. Jesus put the integrity of His life on the line and rested His fate in the hands of the public. But His enemies brought false charges against Him, and when given the choice between Jesus and Barabbas, the public chose a convicted criminal over the innocent Jesus. It was this kind of a risk that Job was willing to take.

The List of Accusations

We've seen that Job has been accused throughout this discussion with his friends of just about every form of human sin—lust, deceit, covetousness, discrimination, neglect, greed, idolatry, vengeance, and selfishness. But as the discussion has evolved we noticed that Eliphaz in his last speech admitted that Job was a righteous man—outwardly. But to justify his belief in the prevailing doctrine of justice he had to identify sin in some form as the cause of Job's suffering so he accused him of the secret sins of the rich and famous. It is these so-called "heart sins" that Job is willing to put on the placard that he will wear in public.

The "heart sins" or secret sins Job lists run something like this—looking at a woman with lust

(31:1–4) . . . being deceitful (31:5–8) . . . coveting a neighbor's wife (31:9–12) . . . oppressing his servants (31:13–15) . . . forgetting the poor, the widows, and orphans (31:16–23) . . . trusting in wealth (31:24–28) . . . being happy over the misfortune of his enemies (31:29–31) . . . serving second best to strangers (31:31–32).

Now, it is important to understand that in developing this list of "heart sins" Job does not admit to being guilty of any of them. In each case he prefaces his description with the words, "If I have . . ." Sins of this kind are hard to prove and hard to deny. Yet Job insists that he hasn't tried to cover up his sins as Adam did (31:33). He has no fear of public exposure, so before God and man he affixes his signature to the list on the placard, willing to wait the verdict. He knows deep inside he is not guilty.

The Sin of Arrogance

Having taken that bold step, Job next turns to God and makes one more impassioned plea for a hearing and for understanding, "Oh that one would hear me! behold, my desire is, that the Almighty would answer me" (31:35). Then Job gets carried away as he reacts to Bildad's description of him as a worm. Instead Job exalts himself as a son of man who sees himself entering into the presence of God, "As a prince I would go near him" (31:37).

Bildad's name-calling had struck a raw nerve. It had pushed Job to one extreme, and now we see him reacting from the other extreme. Human nature had won out, for while Job can't be accused of other outward or inward sins, he is now guilty of the sin of arrogance.

Finally, almost as an afterthought, Job adds one more "sin of the heart" to his list of possible accusations (31:38–40). In the rugged country east of the Jordan River good farm and pasture land was scarce. To waste or rape the land was an unforgivable sin. So Job throws out another "If" challenge as he dares anyone to accuse him of doing anything that would damage the land in a way that would reduce the production of food on which their survival depended.

It would appear that Job passed the test of character. His integrity was intact with both God and his fellowmen. The only shadow that discolors the scene at all is the arrogance which makes him think that he can prance into the presence of God like a prince before a king. Servant he is; prince he is not!

The closing words of Chapter 31 speak volumes, "The words of Job are ended." He has said it all. Throughout this long discussion with Eliphaz, Bildad, and Zophar he has wrestled with the religious thinking of his time. He has agonized over the criticism of his friends, even as he has struggled with God's silence. Through it all Job felt very much alone. Yet he remained convinced that he was not guilty of sin even though he suffered the loss of social position, of family, and of personal wealth. Somehow his faith in God—a personal God—remained intact.

As we reflect on our lessons so far, there are many practical lessons we twentieth-century Christians can learn from the Job story. Even though Job was a man of his time with all of the ambiguities in his understanding of God, he models for us a steadiness of faith which we need for our time. There is so much that happens we don't understand. Our television screens bring pictures of emaciated babies starving to death in Third World countries. Our papers give notice of young people in their twenties and thirties whose lives are ended through tragic accidents or disease. We read of brutal genocide in Vietnam and Cambodia—and we look up into the heavens and ask why. As with Job, there is so much we don't understand, but *with* Job we can say with confidence, "Though he slay me, yet will I trust in him" (13:15). And with that trust comes an inner peace that brings healing.

As we reflect on the discussions—debates—between Job and his three friends, we're reminded of the saying, "With friends like that, who needs enemies." It's easy to be critical of Eliphaz, Bildad, and Zophar. But even though they were wrong, we have to think they were sincere in holding to what they believed to be true. They were so convinced they were right that they failed to be sensitive to the voice

The Last Word

and feelings of Job. They refused to hear him because of their own prejudices and their sense of being *so right.* In their blindness they were guilty of playing God.

This, too, sends up a warning flag for us to be sensitive to the needs of our friends and constantly open to the voice of the Holy Spirit.

Father God, Help me to see Your hand controlling the events of my life—and when I cannot see, help me to trust that You are still God, that nothing escapes You. AMEN.

WHAT THIS SCRIPTURE MEANS TO ME
Job 22:1—31:40

The gnarled hands whittled away at the small piece of wood. The artisan knew exactly where to put his knife and exactly how much pressure to exert to carve out his idea in wood. With the sensitivity born of much experience, he knew when to turn the wood to make his creation come out just right.

Life had carved its own artistry on his face; laugh lines played on the same face beside deep crevices of pain. I had seen both tears of sorrow and tears of joy course down those wrinkles.

Taking a deep breath to build my courage, I brought up the subject of strength. I asked my friend to tell me how he had come to such peace, and then I hoped I hadn't probed in places I didn't belong.

"You see," he replied, "I've had one big problem 'most all my life. I couldn't believe it when it showed up, because it was the one thing I said I'd never have."

I wanted to know what the "big problem" was, but something kept me silent. Maybe he would tell me. Maybe it didn't matter what it was.

"Yes, sir," he said to me. "I begged God over and over to take that problem away from me. I tried to deny that it belonged to me. I hoped it would disappear some night and I wouldn't ever have to wake up to it again. I tried running away from it. I tried to blame other folks. I bargained with God, making all sorts of promises if He would fix me. I wanted God to take my problem away, but He didn't see fit to do that."

"Now I see that I was lucky to have to carry this burden through the years. If it hadn't been for it, I wouldn't ever have found God."

I knew the words were not empty words, but words backed up with years of struggle and pain. The strength and serenity I saw had nothing to do with cheap grace. I knew that the battle he had fought with his stubborn will had cost him much.

"It's an awesome thing to fall into the hands of God," he continued. "What I discovered was that the only reason I was able to find God was that He had already found me, and that happened because of my problem."

I find it hard, in the middle of wrestling with a problem, to see that the problems I have may be a vehicle of grace. Early on, my tendency is to appoint myself judge over the situation, casting my opinion as to whether or not something is good or bad, fair or unfair.

With a little life under my belt, I'm learning that it is counterproductive to make pronouncements on situations until all the facts are in. There isn't any point in calling a score until the game is over.

My friend had come face to face with that which he could not change. He had, through testing his mettle and earning his stripes, come to change that which he could change. Through his lifetime, he had come to know the difference between what he could change and what he could not, and in the process, had come to serenity, courage, and wisdom. And if he hadn't had that journey, he might never have learned first-hand about grace and mercy.

"Everybody has something," my woodcarver-sage continued. "Everybody has his own row to hoe, his own solitary battle to fight. It ain't what happens to you that makes you strong or weak, but how you take it."

Job expressed the same kind of confidence in the processes of God, and his faith is recorded in Job 23:10. "But he knoweth the way that I take: when he hath tried me, I shall come forth as gold."

LESSON 6
JOB 32:1–37:24

The Test of Truth

Father God, Thank You for Your truth, which sets me free—free from the lies and snares of the evil one, free to be who I really am, free to obey and serve You. AMEN.

Our Scripture lesson opens in a vacuum of silence. The Job writer puts it this way, "So these three men ceased to answer Job, because he was righteous in his own eyes [he continued to believe he was without fault]" (32:1). Now we learn that there has been a fourth person listening to the discussion or debate—a young man named Elihu. It is obvious this young man has a spiritual heritage because his name means "He is my God." We're also told that he is the son of Barachel, whose name means "God has blessed." From that description it is likely that Elihu was from a wealthy family.

The Job writer also explains that Elihu was a Buzite (32:2a). A study of the genealogy of that time reveals that Buz was a brother of Uz, which would make him one of Job's ancestors. All of this adds up to the fact that in some way Elihu was related to Job. This may possibly account for his presence throughout the discussion.

It is apparent that young Elihu was a student at the

Wisdom School. At any rate, he had been listening to the back-and-forth arguments and comments of Eliphaz, Bildad, Zophar, and Job. And as he listened, he had become very upset and angry—both at Job and at the other three men. We'll soon learn from what he says that he was completely disillusioned because four of the wisest and most respected men in the ancient East were caught in the grips of an irreconcilable argument which had gone past the point of reason. As he saw it, the attitude of these older wise men canceled out all they had taught him.

Adult leaders whose practice contradicts their teaching always incite their young followers to anger and disillusionment. When their heroes or their idealism is crushed, young people become confused and angry. And apparently young Elihu's emotions had gone the full cycle while listening to the discussion— from awe to disappointment and from disillusionment to white-hot anger.

Elihu's Right to Speak (32:1–22)
A Time for Anger

While youthful anger is often helter-skelter and undisciplined, this wasn't true in Elihu's case. The reason for his anger was very personal. He was angry with Job because he justified himself while blaming God—he insisted he was righteous but still seemed to blame God for what had happened to him (32:2). At the same time young Elihu was angry at Eliphaz, Bildad, and Zophar because they continued to believe Job was guilty of sin even though they had no proof of it (32:3).

It would be easy for us to write Elihu off because he is young and angry. As we follow his remarks, we will see that he is also repetitious and even boring. But as the story unravels, we will see that he plays an indispensable role in preparing the way for Job's ultimate personal encounter with God. A person in Elihu's role is always needed when disagreement and conflict lead to a stalemate rather than reconciliation. Experience indicates that as a rule only intervention from some outside source can lead to the resolving of a stalemate of any kind.

The Bible gives us a clear pattern for resolving conflicts among Christians. Knowing that situations would arise when persons in the church are unable to agree, the Apostle Paul provided an agenda for such times. He prohibited people who were locked in what seemed to be an irreconcilable conflict from going into secular courts for arbitration. Instead he proposed a process of intervention that might lead to reconciliation. The disagreeing parties should first bring in a mediator from within the congregation. If the mediator failed, then the conflict would be taken to the elders in the church who would then make a decision that was binding on all parties. To those of us who live in a litigious time when bringing legal action in the courts as a means of solving conflict is so popular, we would do well to pay closer attention to the biblical model as a part of our Christian witness in a secular society.

Young, But Honest

Elihu's introductory remarks are almost better than anything else he says. This reminds me of a comment made by a friend of mine who is a master at public speaking, "People remember introductions as much as the speech. If you identify with your listeners and create an air of anticipation in your introduction, people won't forget it."

Elihu's honesty comes through clearly when he begins by saying, "I am young, and ye are very old; wherefore I was afraid, and durst not shew you mine opinion" (32:6). With these words, he has won the respect of his hearers. He readily acknowledges his youth and inexperience while at the same time recognizing the knowledge and experience of the older men in the circle. Yes, he has been moved to anger over what he has heard, but Elihu is no wild-eyed kid who thinks he knows it all.

Honesty is disarming. This is well illustrated by the success of two television personalities, Johnny Carson and Pat Robertson. Each of them has the disarming grin of a kid caught with his hand in the cookie jar, the stuttering style of an uncertain communicator, and an air of humility with which we identify. Yet, behind their grin, stutter, and appearance of humility is an uncanny sense of timing and total control of their situation. Whether in the comedian's opening monologue or the preacher's closing homily, they each reinforce their image and

The Breath of the Almighty

identify with their audience. And the result? High ratings.

Having established his identity as young and fearful, Elihu expresses his disappointment in the failure of his elders to speak words of wisdom. Against their failure, then, he extends his own credibility for speaking by suggesting that the "inspiration [breath] of the Almighty" is not limited by age or experience (32:8). Here is a gritty indictment of his elders. Elihu challenges the authority of age as the source of wisdom. How true! The "breath of the Almighty" is a gift of God that is not preferential to age. "Out of the mouths of babes come words of wisdom" is a truth that we cannot ignore.

Our daughter, Debra, was only four years old when we took her to a church service in which the pastor invited those who wanted to receive Jesus Christ as their personal Savior to come forward and pray at the altar. A friend of ours went to the altar to weep and struggle for an hour without apparent relief. Debra sat in the front seat with her crayons and coloring book as we stayed with him to pray. On the way home, I remarked to my wife, "John finds it hard to become a Christian." From the back seat, a little voice piped up, "What's the matter? Doesn't he love Jesus?" Then and there, I realized what Jesus meant when He said that we had to become as little children to enter the Kingdom of Heaven.

On another occasion, our college sophomore son returned home for vacation. The telephone began to ring incessantly as his high school friends called him for parties and reunions. One night, though, a very special invitation came from a girl Rob had idealized as the beauty of the high school. Rob accepted the invitation and left the house with eager anticipation.

The next day, we asked him how things went. "I didn't like what I saw," he answered. "Some Christian kids may go wild, but they still have a base." Then he told us that his high school dreamboat had changed in the two years since graduation. Their values had grown apart—he toward his friends in the

Christian college, she toward her sisters in a college sorority. Rob's wisdom in sorting out the difference and making a choice amazed us.

With the "inspiration [breath] of the Almighty" as his claim to credibility, Elihu now proceeds to explain the spirit with which he speaks—with a *patient* spirit—"I waited for your words" (32:11) . . . with a *discerning* spirit—"I gave ear to your reasons" (32:11) . . . with an *attentive* spirit—"I attended unto you" (32:12).

Earning the Right to Speak

Certainly, with this kind of insight and attitude no one can ever accuse Elihu of being a wild-eyed radical, even though he may seem to be mad at the world. Without question he has earned his right to speak. And because Eliphaz, Bildad, and Zophar have not been successful in their arguments and responses to Job, he believes he is free to enter the discussion.

Still humble to the point of being apologetic, Elihu refuses to get bogged down in the arguments that produced the stalemate. So he now makes it clear that he will not condemn Job with the same words and ideas they used, but will speak for himself (32:14–16); that he will speak with passion (32:18–20); and above all, he won't show partiality or resort to flattery (32:21). In other words, in spite of his youth and lack of experience, he will be himself, with his inspiration coming from the Lord. His words and his spirit demonstrate the importance of what he has to say.

Throughout all of these opening comments not one of the older men interrupted young Elihu. They listened respectfully in silence, possibly aware somehow that although their young student didn't have the years of experience and maturity they had, he should be listened to. Their apparent attitude illuminates an important truth. Effective communication in the home, in the office or store, or in church is a two-way street. Yes, youth should listen to and learn from those who are older and more mature. But youth should be listened to as well. No one—young or old—should be written off as lacking insight and wisdom.

**The Spirit of
Understanding (33:1–33)**

With the stage set, Elihu first directs his attention to Job (33:1–7). In these opening remarks Elihu pleads with Job to listen to him because he is going to speak candidly and honestly. He also points out that while he is a man just like Job, the Spirit of the Lord—the breath of God—is with him.

Next, Elihu reminds Job that in his earlier discussions he had expressed three complaints against God. First, Job had defended his own innocence (33:8–9); second, Job had claimed that his suffering was unjust (33:10–11); and third, Job had contended that God's silence was proof that He doesn't care about him (33:10–11).

Speaking Truth in Love

As we listen attentively to Elihu's opening words to Job, we catch the tone of an earnest young man who wants desperately to be understood. His words bring to mind the Apostle Paul's commendation for "speaking the truth in love" (Eph. 4:15). Most certainly, the delicate balance of truth and love becomes possible for any of us only when we speak with the "breath of the Almighty"—under the guidance of the Holy Spirit. Otherwise we err toward one extreme or the other—unfeeling truth or soggy love. It is only when truth and love are balanced and fused by the Spirit of God that our spirits are right and we can be of help and guidance to others.

Tactful, Yet Honest

Elihu's ability to balance truth and love is clearly seen as he refutes Job's complaints against God. In responding to Job's claim of being innocent and without fault (33:9) Elihu refers to what he understood Job to say about God's unjust treatment of him in spite of his innocence, "Behold, he findeth occasions against me [criticizes or finds fault with me], he counteth me [treats me like] his enemy, He putteth my feet in stocks [He confines my feet], he marketh all my paths [He watches everything I do]" (33:10–11).

After quoting or paraphrasing Job's accusation against God, Elihu then tells him that is where he is wrong, "Behold, in this thou art not just [right]"

(33:12a). Because of this, he is not innocent but is guilty of sin—the sin of arrogance.

In response to Job's contention that God's silence is a sign of indifference, Elihu reminds him that God speaks in many different ways, including dreams and visions (33:14–16). This reminder must have stung Job, because up until now he had insisted that God answer him on his own terms—face-to-face and point-by-point in something like a courtroom setting. On the contrary, dreams and visions are not that straightforward but are composed of symbols that can only be understood by intuition.

Modern research reveals different functions for the right and left side of the human brain. The left side controls rational thinking, whereas intuitive perceptions center in the right side. Truth can be discovered either way—by reason or intuition—but there needs to be a balance. Job in his search for truth

Learning through Intuition

Undoubtedly, the harshness of the setting—like what is pictured below—the self-righteous criticism of Job's three friends, and now being told by young Elihu that he is guilty of sin had plunged Job into the depths of despair. Yet, somehow, he held on to his faith in God in the midst of his questions.

would be diagnosed as a left brain person. But now Elihu seems to be suggesting that he needs to develop the right side of his brain also.

The point being made is that God has something to teach Job about sin and pride through his intuition as well as his reason, and all of his experience is a part of God's plan to save him (33:17–18). In other words, through suffering which cannot be understood by reason, God wants Job to learn that there is more than one way of knowing truth and gaining wisdom.

It is dreadfully easy for us to be critical of Job as we work our way through these lessons. It is true that probably none of us has suffered the losses Job had, but from our vantage point we could likely think that, among other things, he should have known better than to expect God to speak to him only on his own terms. Yet, how often we're guilty, one way or another, of the same thing. When we have a special need, we think God ought to meet it *our* way and in *our* timing. And if He doesn't produce the way we see it, we start complaining and asking why. We rebel against the advice of the Wisdom writer who said, "Trust in the Lord with all thine heart; *and lean not unto thine own understanding*" (Prov. 3:5, italics mine).

Learning through Pain

Undoubtedly, truth stings again when Elihu suggests that pain may also be a way of God's teaching (33:19). We avoid this truth for fear that we will equate pain and learning as God's only purpose for suffering. Yet, without falling into that trap, we cannot deny the truth that learning wisdom is painful. Some educators go so far as to say that without pain there is no learning. As radical as that idea may seem, we must admit that our most significant learning experiences come, not when we are calm and comfortable, but when we are struggling through some kind of hard times or suffering.

Possibly God's Preventative

In this part of our Scripture lesson, too, Elihu takes a bold step in turning his attention to the perennial question, "Why do the innocent suffer?" In response he suggests that pain and suffering may be the preventative that God uses to keep us from going down into the pit of death and destruction (33:18–19). We say a great deal about God's saving grace, but we place all too little emphasis on the grace of God that works in us each day "preventing" us from committing spiritual suicide.

As Christians we live an hour at a time and a day at a time by the keeping and sustaining grace of God. He not only saves us; He keeps us. It is His gift of grace to us.

Why doesn't Job react violently now as Elihu has suggested that God may be teaching him *through* his suffering? After all, When Eliphaz suggested the same idea, Job flew into a rage. But the difference is in Elihu's tone and spirit. Elihu sees the purpose of Job's suffering as redemptive—not punitive as Eliphaz had.

Above all, though, with prophetic insight Elihu appears to look ahead across the centuries as he offers the promise of a Mediator, "one among a thousand," who will show Job not only the justice of God but also His grace through a ransom that will deliver Job's soul "from going down to the pit" (33:23–24).

There can be no doubt about the spirit with which Elihu is speaking. In some mysterious way he is a prophet who foresees Jesus Christ as the Mediator between God and people as well as the Savior who ransoms the human soul through His own suffering. In Christ, the balance between truth and love is personified.

Now, Elihu's expression of God's promise makes sense, "His flesh shall be fresher than a child's: he [Job] shall return to the days of his youth" (33:25). In other words, he will be restored to his youthful vigor—because of the Redeemer's ransom and not because of anything Job does or has done. Inspired by the "breath of the Almighty," Elihu has foreseen the "new creation" in Christ Jesus of whom Paul wrote (2 Cor. 5:17).

All of Job's complaints against God fall like dominoes under Elihu's word of truth spoken in love. God is not silent; He speaks in many different ways which Job needs to hear. God is not unjust in permitting Job to suffer; He wants to teach Job the discipline of pain

The Breath of the Almighty

and prevent him from falling into the pit of death and destruction. And most of all, God is not indifferent to Job's suffering. Graciously and patiently, He comes to Job time and time again with a Mediator of truth and a Savior of love to ransom him from the captivity of sin.

Job Has Met His Match

Inspired by the Spirit of God, Elihu has given us a glimpse of God that matches Job's vision of the living Redeemer (19:25). To Elihu, God is a creative teacher who speaks in many ways, a watchful guardian who keeps us from destroying ourselves, a living Redeemer who gives Himself as our ransom, and a patient friend who forgives us time and time again (33:24–30).

Yes, Job has met his match. When Elihu invites him to speak, the man who proudly said he would enter the presence of God like a prince before the king, falls silent for the first time. At the feet of a young man, in a scene which shatters all the tradition of the ancient East, we see Job ready to obey when Elihu reverses his role as a silent bystander and says to his elder, "Harken unto me: hold thy peace, *and I shall teach thee wisdom*" (33:33, italics mine).

The Ear of Reason (34:1–37)
Elihu Speaks to Eliphaz, Bildad, and Zophar

Abruptly and without warning, Elihu turns from Job to Eliphaz, Bildad, and Zophar. With an air of disdain he calls them to attention. "Hear my words, O ye wise men; and give ear to me [listen to me], ye that have knowledge [you wise men]. For the ear trieth words, as the mouth tasteth meat [for the ear examines what is said as the mouth tastes food]" (34:2–3).

Not only has Elihu changed his tone, but he has also changed the source of his authority. Earlier he had spoken to Job with the "spirit of understanding and the breath of the Almighty." Now he appeals to the "ear" of his hearers. In biblical symbolism, the ear represents human reason and the logical process by which we know and test the truth.

The Scales of Justice

Why the sudden change of audience, tone, and authority? Is Elihu mimicking his elders? Certainly there is some value in having them hear themselves talk, not with the gentle and reasoned tone of wisdom, but with the harsh and defensive tone of anger.

Elihu may have had that motive in the back of his mind, but he had a nobler purpose. His subject is now the justice of God that stands over against the grace of God of which he has just spoken. Like a judge weighing law and grace on the scales of justice, Elihu argues both sides of the case.

By balancing justice and grace, Elihu is staying true to his promise to speak impartially and without flattery to both parties. Having spoken the truth in love to Job, he now takes on the role of speaking with cold and hard reason—the language of the inner ear. Perhaps he wants to teach Job the contrast between the God of grace and the God of justice in dealing with his sins.

Elihu's Challenge

Very early in this speech Elihu quotes Job as he issues his challenge, "Let us choose to us judgment [let us decide for ourselves what is right]: let us know among ourselves what is good. For Job hath said, I am righteous: and God hath taken away my judgment [God has denied me justice]. Should I lie against my right? my wound is incurable without transgression [I'm not guilty of anything but I am deeply wounded]" (34:4–6).

Rather than just accepting outright Job's interpretation of what is just and unjust, Elihu urges his hearers to make their own decision after he has presented his arguments for the justice of God. But in quoting Job as he has, Elihu appears to take liberty with what Job has actually said throughout their long discussion and debate. Under the weight of his suffering and agony, Job has come close to saying "I am righteous, and God is not just or fair"—but he hasn't quite said it as blatantly as Elihu puts it now. But at this point Elihu has positioned Job as being against God. In doing so he has sided with Eliphaz, Bildad, and Zophar.

Job Is Accused Falsely

Elihu then sarcastically sneers, "What man is like Job who drinketh up scorning like water?" (34:7). With these words Elihu is accusing Job of being scornful of God, of scoffing at God and the religious thinking of that time. By complaining about the "injustice" of God, Job has joined the company of "the workers of iniquity" and "wicked men" (34:7–8). This was a false accusation because nothing in our story indicates that Job kept company with sinful people. Yes, he was guilty of pride and arrogance but not of moral sin.

Next Elihu puts words into Job's mouth when he accuses Job of saying, "It profiteth a man nothing that he should delight himself in the Lord" (34:9). At no time has Job been so rash as to equate "delight" in the Lord with "profit." If Job had served God only for the benefits he had received, then Satan would have been right when he sneered, "Does Job serve God for naught?"

Most certainly Job had not been guilty of the sin of using God or of trying to manipulate Him. The modern counterpart to this attitude can be seen in the businessman who attends church in order to attract business from the congregation—or the professional person who is seen every Sunday morning in the prestigious church of the community's "movers and shakers"—the church attended by the "right" people.

Don't lose track of the setting for Elihu's remarks at this time. Actually, he is addressing himself to Eliphaz, Bildad, and Zophar, but he's quoting Job at times, and what he's saying is not just directed toward the three men but indirectly toward Job.

Elihu Defends God's Impartiality

Elihu moves on now in his defense of the justice of God as he says, "Therefore hearken unto me [listen to me], ye men of understanding [you wise men]: far be it from God, that he should do wickedness [act in an evil way]; and from the Almighty, that he should commit iniquity [do wrong]" (34:10).

Coming at the question of God's justice from yet another angle, Elihu now speaks at length in defence of God's fairness and impartiality. But at best his arguments are confusing. On one hand he insists God is fair and impartial in His actions toward kings and princes and ordinary citizens, toward the rich and the poor, and toward those who are powerful and those who are not (34:18–20).

But then on the other hand, he says that those who disobey God and are hypocritical will not escape the swift and sure judgment of God for their actions (34:22–32). And that assertion is followed immediately with the statement that God is not obligated to dispense His judgment on our terms (34:33). This was certainly a direct dig at Job who earlier had begged God to either strike him dead if he was guilty of sin or restore his health and wealth if he were righteous.

At this point Elihu once again turns to Job and invites him to respond to what has been said (34:33b). But evidently the air is heavy with silence. Job, for whatever reason, offers no defense against the accusations that have been hurled against him by his angry and disturbed young kinsman.

Job Remains Silent

Throughout Elihu's lengthy and confusing speech Job has felt the full force of the young man's contempt for his insisting on his innocence from moral sins. Certainly no one could accuse Elihu of being partial in his arguments—he has condemned Job for insisting he is righteous before God, and with equal fervor he has embarrassed Eliphaz, Bildad, and Zophar by identifying Job's sin as arrogance and pride when they had been unable to perceive the truth.

Job's silence seems to have caused Elihu to become increasingly disturbed, because next he asks Eliphaz, Bildad, and Zophar to listen carefully to what he now wants to say. When he is sure he has their attention, he accuses Job of speaking without knowledge and of using words that do not contain wisdom (34:34–35). This is a strong indictment against Job, but it is interesting to note that Elihu is condemning Job's words and not his character.

Words . . . without Wisdom

Let's pause for a moment and move in for a closer look at the difference between Elihu's forceful condemnation of Job and the attack staged against him by Eliphaz, Bildad, and Zophar. It seems to me that the major difference is one of tone. Yes, Elihu is affronted and angry with Job, but the other three were downright hateful. Elihu has condemned Job's

Contrasting Attitudes

123

pride and arrogance with anger but without attempting to destroy him completely. On the other hand Eliphaz and company were vicious as they first accused Job of being wicked, then evil, and finally they called him a worm—a crushing indictment aimed at destroying Job's spirit and manhood completely.

A teacher of teachers once told his class, "If Johnny steals a pencil, don't call him a thief. Instead deal with the fact that Johnny stole a pencil. More often than not you will solve the problem and save the boy."

This is wise advice for all of us. We have a tendency when involved in a dispute or with a difficult problem to resort to setting up stereotypes. Then we stoop to name-calling and applying labels—liberal, conservative, white, black, Bible-believing, heretic. We find it easy and convenient to put other people into pigeonholes of our own making and so become terribly subjective. Fortunately, in spite of Elihu's passion he remains objective.

The Wrong-Headedness of Pride (35:1–16)

As Elihu assesses the situation, he believes that Job's pride has not only moved him into the company of undesirable people, but has also given him a distorted view of God. Then it would appear that Elihu either misquotes Job or puts words into his mouth when he says, "For thou saidest, What advantage will it be unto thee? and, what profit shall I have if I be cleansed from my sin?" (35:3). Elihu is accusing Job of saying here, "Why should I be good anyway because God doesn't hear and answer my prayer?" Sounds familiar, doesn't it?

Wrong-Headed Thinking

As Elihu is interpreting Job's thinking, he concludes that Job's concept of God is all wrong. Elihu then goes on to remind Job that God is not dependent on the action or reaction of His creation, whether sinful or righteous. After all, if we sin, that doesn't make God less holy, and if we are righteous that doesn't make Him more holy.

At the same time, our sin or righteousness is not without consequences. Even though God's character or nature may not be affected, our sin or righteousness affects us personally as well as all the rest of society. When we sin, other people are hurt, and when we live righteously, other people are blessed (35:5–8).

Millions of people in our society today abuse their bodies, minds, and souls because of their dependency on alcohol, drugs, and other chemicals. They assume falsely that they are only hurting themselves. But studies of substance abuse show that every person who is dependent on alcohol, drugs, or other chemicals hurts at least three other people. In reality, there is no such thing as "private" sin when it comes to consequences. What we do, how we live, produces a chain reaction that affects many other people.

Wrong-Headed Prayers

But there's more, (as Elihu moves ahead and warns that pride causes people to pray wrong-headed prayers.) He illuminates the truth that we usually pray only for relief when we suffer or are oppressed (35:9). Instead, though, Elihu reminds Job that the primary purpose of prayer is to enter into the presence of God. "Where is God my maker, who giveth songs in the night?" is the prayer of worship that is intended to precede our petitions. This pattern is clear in the prayer Jesus taught, "Our Father which art in heaven, Hallowed be thy name. Thy kingdom come. Thy will be done in earth, as it is in heaven" (Matt. 6:9–10). These are all words of worship that precede the first petition—"Give us this day our daily bread."

But wrong-headed praying, so common to all of us, reverses the order. We pray first for relief from suffering or ask for our daily bread. Worship comes last, if at all. When we reverse the true order of prayer, we miss what God has for us, for He wants to give us "songs in the night"; He wants to teach us "more than the beasts of the earth" and make "us wiser than the fowls [birds] of heaven" (35:10–11).

Elihu is saying here that there are greater answers to prayer than relief from suffering. Only God can give us a song to sing in the night of our suffering. Only God can teach us to understand the meaning of suffering beyond the base instinct of animals. And only God can help us see suffering and life's hard times from the perspective of His purpose for the wholeness of life. But we only receive these answers when we move into the realm of God's presence.

It is pride that causes us to pray selfishly. And Elihu warns Job that he shouldn't be surprised when God doesn't listen to his pleas for relief or respond to his demands that God appear before him and defend Himself against Job's accusations (35:12–16). Again, I'm sure that as each of us reflects on our own prayer life, we, like Job, are speechless. So often our prayers take on a selfish note. We pray when we want something or are threatened in some way, but when things are running smoothly, we become careless and take God for granted. Yet, how much stronger our spiritual life would be if we, like the Psalmist, would regularly "Give thanks [and praise] unto the Lord, for he is good: for his mercy endureth for ever" (Psa. 107:1).

God Is Good; God Is Great (36:1–37:24)

Before going on, Elihu apologizes for the length of his speech but asks Job to bear with him a little longer (36:1). Still assuming the role of the teacher, Elihu once again gives us the source of his authority before proceeding. He states boldly that his knowledge comes from far and wide—from many sources—and that wisdom and justice come from God (36:2–3).

Earlier, Elihu spoke with the "breath of the Almighty" when he revealed the grace of God. Later, he spoke through the "ear of reason" when he defended the justice of God. Now both the Spirit of Grace and the Letter of the Law come together in a review of God's work throughout human history.

The Goodness of God

True to his role as a teacher, Elihu next states very simply the subject of the next lesson he wants to get across, "Behold, God is mighty, and despiseth not any: he is mighty in strength and wisdom" (36:5). Rather than thinking of the awesome power of God which arbitrarily overwhelms us as Job has claimed, Elihu speaks of the strength of God's understanding. Then he reminds Job that God always keeps the righteous in His sight (36:7). If they are afflicted, He uses suffering to save them from past sin and turn them from future sin (36:9–10). And on such occasions, they have three choices: they can obey God and be restored; they can reject God and be destroyed; or they can play God and become perverted (36:11–15).

Job's Real Problem

For the first time, now, Elihu appears to point his finger directly at Job and in effect say, "You are the man." Evidently Job's wealth and his feelings of being right had become a hindrance. His wealth had made him so self-sufficient that he didn't think he really needed God, and his being so right had made him so "holy" that he didn't think he needed full salvation—his spiritual self-sufficiency was leading him toward sin. For this reason, God was permitting him to suffer, in order to turn him away from sin and teach him to trust, not on riches or righteousness, but on God alone, "Behold, God exalteth by his power [God is exalted]: who teacheth like him? Who hath enjoined him his way? Or who can say, Thou hast wrought iniquity [No one can tell God what to do or charge Him with being evil]" (36:22–23).

In human terms, power corrupts and absolute power corrupts absolutely. But God is just the opposite. His absolute power glorifies Him because His purpose is always good.

The Greatness of God

Next, we see Elihu shifting the focus of his teaching from human history to natural history, "Remember that thou magnify his work [remember to celebrate God's work], which men behold. Every man may see it; man may behold it afar off [everyone has seen it, but we can only look from a distance]" (36:24–25).

As Elihu visualizes the world around him, he sees all of nature validating his arguments. Looking far off across the desert he sees the storm clouds forming. Thunder rumbles in the distance and lightning splits the sky (36:26–33). In the power of the approaching storm Elihu senses that God is near, and he says, "At this also my heart trembleth, and is moved out of his place [my heart beats rapidly]" (37:1). His heart is pounding and his pulse has quickened as he views the strength of God's power in the storm.

In awe and with a fresh flood of inspiration Elihu likens the thunder to God's majestic voice. And through His voice God issues instructions on the flow of the seasons and the meaning of the elements: the snow, the gentle rain, the heavy rain, the whirlwind, the scattering winds, the ice, the frozen seas, the thick clouds, and the bright clouds. All of these respond to the will of God.

What is Elihu trying to say? The message is clear. All of creation—all of nature—is under God's control and moves in line with His purpose. "He causeth it to come, whether for correction, or for his land, or for mercy" (37:13). All of this gives testimony to the greatness and the reliability of God and reminds us of the Psalmist's magnificent hymn of praise, "The earth is the Lord's, and the fulness thereof; the world and they that dwell therein. For he hath founded it upon the seas, and established it upon the floods" (Psa. 24:1–2). This is the God we can count on even in life's most perplexing moments!

Elihu has now given a new and fresh insight into God's purposes. Both in natural creation and in His human creation we have a vast panorama stretching across all of history that portrays the greatness and the goodness of God. Take the rain for example. Sometimes it rains to give relief from drought, sometimes it rains to beautify the earth, and sometimes it rains as an act of mercy. Whichever the case may be, God's purpose is good.

Worship God in His Majesty

With the passing of the storm, Elihu captures the meaning of the moment as he calls Job to "stand still, and consider the wondrous works of God" (37:14). The clouds are shining and making patterns in the sky. A south wind blows, the sun breaks through with blinding brilliance, and golden splendor spreads across the northern skies—God is there!

Then in the midst of this majesty Elihu leaves Job with some unanswered questions: Do you know *when* God sends His wondrous works and *what* causes the light in His clouds to shine? (37:15); do you know *how* the clouds hang the way they do? (37:16); do you know *why* your clothes are warm? (37:17); do you know *who* spreads out the skies? (37:18).

The "when," "what," "how," "why," and "who" all point to a mighty Creator-God and testify to His majesty and greatness. As I've stood on the south rim of the Grand Canyon or walked along the rugged Washington and Oregon coast or paused in the midst of the awesome grandeur of the Rocky Mountains or traveled along the rocky New England coast, I have felt my heart pound and my pulse quicken as I have reflected on the work of God. At such moments any pride or arrogance has given way to my sense of smallness in contrast to the grandeur of God's creation. Somehow in such moments "why?" seems irrelevant.

Elihu's Job Is Finished

Elihu's work is done. He began his lecture to Eliphaz, Bildad, Zophar, and Job with angry criticism and sarcasm; he closes with gentle teaching. Like John the Baptist who had the privilege of preparing the way and announcing the coming of Jesus Christ, Elihu, as we shall see, has prepared the way and announced the coming of God Almighty.

Just as John the Baptist introduced the Lamb of God who would take away the sin of the world, Elihu announced that God comes in golden splendor, in awesome majesty, and in excellent power (37:19–24). As simple as a child's table grace, Elihu has indeed spoken the truth in love—God is great; God is good!

Lord God, I see Your power in a thunderstorm; Your beauty in a baby's smile, Your mystery in the fog. Your creation declares Your glory! Amen.

WHAT THIS SCRIPTURE MEANS TO ME
Job 32:1—37:24

It was one of those cool evenings in the mountains. Stretched and challenged by an afternoon of mountain climbing, my family and I gathered on a Sunday evening to share a family worship.

Earlier, my husband had asked us to look for ways that God would speak to us through nature during our day's sojourn in the valleys and meadows of the high country. None of us was to talk about the discoveries until we returned to the cabin that night. Our findings would be the "sermon" of our evening worship.

Our intent, as very serious and conscientious parents, was to enable our children to see not only the beauty of creation, but to become tuned in to the Creator behind it all. Later, we would move to deeper theological training in matters of the faith, but on this day, we would discuss the basics.

Amy, our youngest daughter, came in with a bucket filled with pebbles which had only moments before been resting in a rushing stream. She took her treasures to the sink, washed them tenderly and then spread them out on the dining table.

As we gathered for our family time, my husband shared how he had been reminded of God by the majesty of the mountain ranges. One daughter had felt God's presence while standing in the tall aspens, while another thought of Him when she saw the playfulness of mountain creatures, scampering to hide themselves from human intruders. I am always brought to my knees by the profusion of beauty in the wildflowers.

When it was Amy's turn, we thought she would make one general statement about her rocks and that would be it. Painstakingly, she took up each little pebble and told us what it represented to her. Each rock had a specific message for her, and so rock after rock, she talked. We older ones began to squirm, wondering how long this sermon might be!

After our prayer time, Amy picked up her rocks and transferred them to the table by her bed. Again, she picked them up, placing them where she could see them as she was going to sleep, so she could "remember how much God loves me."

Later, I reflected on the simple, easy trust of this little child. How willingly she believed that God loved her and was as near to her as her own breath. She hadn't argued with us about whether or not God wanted to communicate with her that day. She hadn't asked us to define the limitations or conditions through which God might get her attention. Neither did she look frantically about from here to there, demanding that God meet her on her terms and on her timetable. She hadn't expected a burning bush, but had accepted what came to her in the simple things.

With the unclouded faith of childhood, Amy went about the business of her day, knowing that she would meet God. She didn't give up on that possibility when she slid down a steep pathway, skinning her hands and muddying her jeans. She didn't rail against God when her sisters teased and bullied her over who would sit where in the Jeep; she didn't conclude that a good God wouldn't let unfairness happen. And she certainly didn't let our restlessness with her lengthy report stymie the message she had received.

Amy's childlike openness has been a message to me about giving up my frantic assaults against the heavens and listening for God's voice in the common, ordinary events of life. Her belief has helped my unbelief when it has seemed that this time God has surely forgotten me or has turned a deaf ear to my need.

I, too, am regaining my childlike faith as I relearn how to lean on God's everlasting arms, assured that "the spirit of God hath made me, and the breath of the Almighty hath given me life."

LESSON 7
JOB 38:1–42:6

The Test of Trust

Lord God, I know my mind can be in perfect peace if I trust in You—no matter what my circumstances suggest, no matter how I feel, no matter the opinions of others—simply trust. *Let me know what it is to trust You.* AMEN.

God in the Whirlwind (38:1–3)

Now, God speaks.

As a final proof that young Elihu spoke with the "breath of the Almighty," the transition between his last words and God's appearance on the scene is as smooth as the adverb which the Job writer uses to introduce the Lord, "*Then* the Lord answered Job out of the whirlwind" (38:1, italics mine). There is no break between the close of Elihu's speech and the first words of the Lord—God immediately takes up where Elihu left off. And He goes on to build on the base of truth that His forerunner had prepared.

Actually, none of us can speak for God, but all of us can prepare the way for Him to speak. Whether we are witnessing, teaching, counseling, or preaching, the test of truth is if there is natural movement from our words to the Word of God. The authenticity of what we say is not determined by the sound or the choice of our words. It isn't a pious tone of voice or the use of "religious language" that gives power to our witness. Rather, it is the presence of God in our words and life that frees us to be forerunners—preparers of the Way. And, certainly, no higher privilege is given to us than to prepare the way for God to speak—to our children and loved ones, to friends and neighbors, to our colleagues, or to our congregations.

Out of the Whirlwind

God's appearance out of a whirlwind did not happen by accident. Anyone who has traveled through the desert will remember the flash storms that come up with deafening thunder, fearful lightning, and drenching rain.

Then, as quickly as it came, the storm passes. Out of the scattering clouds comes sunshine whose brilliance is magnified through the last of the raindrops. The hot south wind returns to sizzle the water on the desert floor, a rainbow with colors mixed on the palette of God arches over the earth, and the peace of heaven settles over the scene. Suddenly, in the distance a swirling cone of dust is spotted. It is a whirlwind in the desert, dancing to its own rhythm with a swoop, a spin, a dash, and a curtsy.

A whirlwind is part of the desert and yet it is not. No one can control its motion or capture its energy, as Jesus noted when He compared the new birth by the Spirit of God with the mystery of the wind, a whirlwind, which "bloweth where it listeth [where it wants to], and thou hearest the sound thereof, but canst not tell whence it cometh, and whither it goeth: so is every one that is born of the Spirit" (John 3:8).

Out of a whirlwind, God speaks to Job. What a difference between God's appearance and Job's expectations. Pride had caused Job to define the ground rules for a meeting with God. He had insisted that God appear as either prosecutor or defendant in a courtroom setting. Intentionally or not, Job had made himself equal with God—ready to ask or answer questions. And he even went farther, putting himself above God. In reality he set the docket—laid out the conditions—for the hearing with the demand that God answer the question, "Why do I suffer?"

Now God ignores Job's arrogant demands. Rather than the orderly procedure of a courtroom, He comes in the swirl of a whirlwind. Rather than answering questions, He asks them. Rather than responding to Job's demand, "Why do I suffer?" God chooses to ask the question, "Who am I?"

The God Who Creates (Job 38:4–21)

Without waiting for an immediate answer the Lord presses on, and no language of Scripture touches the Eternal more than God's rapid-fire questions to Job: "Where wast thou when I laid the foundations of the earth?" (38:4). "Or who shut up the sea with doors . . . ? (38:8). "Hast thou commanded the morning since thy days; and caused the dayspring to know his place . . . ?" (38:12). "Hast thou entered into the springs of the sea?" (38:16). "Where is the way where light dwelleth?" (38:19).

God is not being cruel. But Job has forgotten who he is—a creature, not the Creator. He deserved to be squashed for his arrogance. But no, as Elihu told Job, God is very patient, coming to us time and time again in order to teach us His ways and save us from self-destruction.

When God is finished with His questions, there is no doubt who He is—He and He alone is the Creator of the universe. God leaves Job speechless when He asks, with a touch of irony, "Knowest thou it, because thou wast then born? [But you know all this because you were born at the creation!] or because the number of thy days is great? [and because you have lived so long]" (38:21).

The God Who Guides (Job 38:22–39:30)

When there is no response from Job, God moves from His general creation to His special creation. His first questions were related to the subject of "who created the universe." Now He asks, "Who controls the universe?" The questions refer to three kinds of special creation.

First, there are the *elements* that make up the natural environment—snow, hail, light, wind, water, thunderbolt, rain, dew, ice, and frost (38:22–30). In each case, God asks a question about the control of creation. With an image that could exist only in the mind of God, He introduces these natural elements by asking Job, "Hast thou entered into the treasures of the snow? or hast thou seen the treasures of the hail, Which I have reserved against the time of trouble, against the day of battle and war?" (38:22–23).

God's purpose in asking these questions is not just to puncture the balloon of Job's self-sufficiency. Rather, He wants to drive the point home that He alone is in control of His universe.

Second, God asks questions about the *constellations* in the heavens which control the seasons (38:31–38). Accurate scientific truth is revealed when God identifies the constellations of Pleiades, Orion, Mazzaroth, and the Great Bear (here called Arcturus) with its Cubs. Again, Job remains silent when God asks if he knows and understands the mysterious laws of the heavens which determine the cycle of the seasons.

Coming still closer to home, God's third set of questions focuses on the *animal* world (38:39–39:30). Like a preview of Noah's Ark, twelve different kinds of animals are paraded before Job's eyes with stunning questions that stagger the human mind. In this parade God speaks of the lion, raven, goat, onager, deer, donkey, ox, ostrich, horse, locust, hawk, and eagle. And in describing this part of His creation, God points out that each is fearfully made and wonderfully different. In particular God refers to the hunting strategy of lions, the random search of ravens, the birthtime of wild mountain goats, the scattering of young deer, the freedom of the wild donkey, the incorrigibility of the wild ox, the foolishness of the ostrich, the courage of the horse, the wisdom of the hawk, and the flight of the eagle.

As we read what God says in these verses, we get an amazing picture of the truth that God is not only the creator of these animals, but He cares for each one of them and is attentive to their needs. And this reminds us of the words of Jesus centuries later when He said, "Are not two sparrows sold for a farthing? and one of them shall not fall on the ground without your Father [knowing about it]. But the very hairs of your head are all numbered. Fear ye not therefore, ye are of more value than many sparrows" (Matt. 10:29–31).

Slowly, but surely, God is asking Job to trust Him. He may not be answering Job's question, "Why do

I suffer?" but He is answering the larger and more important question, "Who am I?"

Job Confesses His Arrogance and Ignorance (40:3–5)

God is doing more than putting Job in his place. By asking questions, even those that Job cannot answer, God shows that He respects the dignity and intelligence of His creation. A master teacher is always distinguished by the art of asking questions. Analogies, in particular, draw together the master teacher and the brilliant student. Now we see that Job is quick to grasp the fact that his question is not "Why?" but "Who?" And he is even quicker to learn that the issue is not understanding why he suffers, but trusting in the One who will sustain him in his suffering. By knowing that God has created the universe, controls its forces, and cares for its creatures, Job is now ready to step up to a new level of trust.

Consequently, we are not surprised when Job accepts God's invitation to speak and gives this answer, "Behold, I am vile; what shall I answer thee? [I am not fit or worthy to answer You]. I will lay mine hand upon my mouth. Once have I spoken; but I will not answer: yea, twice; but I will proceed no further [I have spoken twice, but I won't speak again]" (40:4–5).

For the first time, Job confesses the sin of arrogance and then is silent. He is now ready to learn whatever God has to teach him.

The God Who Cares (40:6–41:34)

Out of the whirlwind, God speaks again. Job has confessed his pride. Every spiritual experience begins with such a confession. Jesus Himself announced His coming with the call to repent and believe the Good News. Only when we confess that we are sinners do we open ourselves to the redeeming grace of God. Anyone who tries to shortcircuit the sequence from repentance to belief is guilty of communicating an easy faith that has no cross and needs no Christ.

Before the greatness of God, Job confessed his pride which had been so clearly seen in his wordy rush to question God's justice. He had demanded that God answer the question, "Why do I suffer?" on his own terms. And he had displayed an arrogance that let him think he could enter the presence of God like a prince before the king. But now Job realizes clearly that God is his Creator and his Guide.

Even with this new flood of insight Job still has questions, "Why am I singled out for suffering?" "Why am I afflicted with this kind of suffering?" "Why is my suffering so untimely?" If we're honest, there are times when we, too, wonder whether or not there is a dark corner of the universe that is outside God's understanding, power, or timing. With infinite patience, God now speaks to those questions.

In order to help Job understand, God now invites Job to reverse roles with Him and respond to his own questions. Role playing is an effective technique for helping us understand another person. When employers and employees, husbands and wives, or parents and children reverse their roles and talk to each other, the results are both helpful and threatening. To hear yourself speak the way others hear you is a shock. Married couples will often say, "Do I talk like that?" when husbands speak impatiently and wives respond in nagging tones.

So God wants Job to hear the way his questions sound to Him. And with that, God asks Job what he would do: Would he "disannul my [God's] judgment? [Would he deny that God is just and fair?]" . . . would he condemn God, "that thou mayest be righteous? [would Job say that God is wrong in order to be right himself?]" . . . "Hast thou an arm like God? or canst thou thunder with a voice like him? [Do you question my power and refuse to hear My voice?]" (40:8–9).

Then before responding to those questions God suggests that Job picture himself arrayed in all of God's majesty and splendor—all of the qualities of God's character—and then "cast abroad the rage of thy wrath [turn loose the full fury of your anger]." "Look on every one that is proud [humble the proud person]" and "tread down the wicked in their place [annihilate wicked people]." "Hide them in the dust together; and bind their faces in secret [bury them in a grave]" (40:11–13). Then God adds that if Job can

A Reversal of Roles

handle these kinds of situations and be wise, fair, gentle, and patient, it would be true that Job doesn't need God (40:14).

A Lesson from History

We have to believe that Job was smart enough to get the point immediately. He realizes that in his arrogance he has tried to play God, and he sees that he is in way over his head.

Human history confirms the fact that Christians who arrogantly think they have wisdom, justice, power, and God's timing in acting against evil usually end up creating a greater evil. Whether in the Crusades of almost a thousand years ago when Christians killed for "righteous" cause or in modern politics when Christians connive to impose their beliefs on society, evil is exchanged for evil. I believe it was Daniel Webster who said, "A strong conviction that something must be done is the parent of many bad measures."

This is not to say that Christians—the people of God in the twentieth century—should not be people of strong belief; but when we step across the narrow line and start playing God, we stand the chance of hurting people and hindering the work of the church.

Job had been guilty of questioning God and of wanting to tell Him how and when things should be done. He placed his understanding of things on a par with God's. But now the Almighty is patiently trying to teach Job to trust Him. The wisdom writer gave us the formula for a rich and full life when he wrote, "Trust in the Lord with all thine heart; *and lean not unto thine own understanding*" (Prov. 3:5, italics mine).

The Use of Symbols and Word Pictures

Every great teacher is an artist. Through the use of symbols, analogies, and word pictures a student learns the meaning of ideas, values, and principles. Jesus was a master teacher. He taught by parables and word pictures in teaching the principles of the kingdom of God—the New Society of believers. To some of His hearers, the parables were nothing more than simple stories. To others, His teaching was gibberish. But as Jesus Himself taught in another of His parables, to those whose minds and hearts were ready for the Good News, the seed of truth took root in fertile soil and grew and produced spiritual fruit.

In a similar manner God chose symbols as a means of speaking to Job's questions. After the heavy weight of the philosophical argument in which Job and his friends were entangled, God chose the symbol of a behemoth or a hippopotamus to teach a lesson about His love. Now, to understand what God is doing, close your eyes for a moment and get a good picture of the hippopotamus.

Let's face it, the hippo is about the most unattractive and the most useless of all the animals of God's creation. It's good for nothing—neither for meat nor skin or for work or play. Yet, God proudly claims the hippopotamus as a product of His creation (40:15–18). Then He goes on to tell Job how much He cares for the hippo—keeping him from danger, providing a source of food for him, and giving him a place for play with trees for shade and cool water for refreshment (40:19–22).

The Ugly and the Useless

God had already spoken to Job about the wonders of His creation and the control and care of the animal kingdom. Now He adds new dimensions. First, God reminds Job that He created him along with the hippo (40:15). Second, He surprises Job with the news that the hippo ranks first among the works of God (40:19). He does not mean that Job is of lesser value than a hippo, but He does mean that He puts a priority on protecting the ugliest and most useless monstrosity of all His creation. Who can love a hippo? God does.

One of the symptoms of spiritual pride is taking yourself too seriously. Over the years, I have decided that a sense of humor goes hand in hand with the spirit of holiness. People who have forgotten how to laugh at themselves and with others are miserable company. Just the other day, I heard a preacher say, "If Satan can't keep us from being righteous, he'll try to make us self-righteous."

A Sense of Humor

Job, the epitome of righteousness, had fallen into the trap of self-righteousness. So God shows him how much He loves a hippopotamus to get things into perspective and to get Job laughing again. Just as the hippo may be the most ludicrous of God's creation, Job's self-righteousness is ludicrous and a laughing matter.

Job, the creature, had taken on the air of the Creator; a man had assumed he was equal with God; and a sinner had dared to imply that he could save himself. Job reminds us of the little girl who told her father that she could draw a picture of God. When her father told her that no one really knew what God looked like, she answered, "When I'm done, they will." In effect, Job had drawn God in his own image. Self-righteousness is like a clown—sad and laughable at the same time.

A Model of Trust

God now presses home His point in asking Job to look at the hippopotamus, and He next says, "Behold, he drinketh up a river, and hasteth not [if the river is flooded, he isn't concerned]: he trusteth that he can draw up the Jordan into his mouth [if the Jordan is rushing high, he remains calm]. He taketh it with his eyes: his nose pierceth through snares [can he be captured by the eyes or be caught in a trap by his nose?]" (40:23–24).

As unappealing as the hippo may be, he is a model of simple trust. Though the Jordan River, the symbol of death, rushes over him, he holds his confidence in the Creator. Even if his nose is pierced by a snare, the symbol of suffering, his trust does not waver. Beyond any doubt, Job's self-sufficiency is being shamed by a picture of a hippopotamus who trusts God.

Grace for the Sinful

Contrast is another effective tool that a master teacher uses to make a point. Still utilizing the image of animals, God now shifts from the behemoth or hippopotamus to the leviathan or crocodile (41:1). The two are the extremes of God's creation. While the hippopotamus is docile and trusting, the crocodile is suspicious and vicious. Symbolically, the crocodile personifies evil in the universe.

The Personification of Evil

God now goes to great length and elaborate detail in asking Job to visualize the crocodile. Through a series of questions God reminds Job that the crocodile cannot be caught, controlled, or used by man for any purpose. He is an incorrigible animal. Anyone who has tried to defeat him comes away with the warning, "Lay thine hand upon him, remember the battle, do no more [if you try to hold him, you'll remember and never do it again]" (41:8).

Now, it is obvious that God wants Job to get a new understanding of evil, because He goes into elaborate detail in describing the crocodile, the personification of evil. And we certainly don't need to be an artist to visualize the biological awesomeness of God's description and see in it also a portrayal of one of the most complete pictures of evil in all of the Bible. Notice the colorful description. His parts [legs] are powerful and graceful (41:12); he is so ferocious that he can't be bridled (41:13); his jaws cannot be forced open and his mouth is full of sharp teeth (41:14); the scales on his body are like a coat of armor (41:15–17); his sneezes or snorts throw out bright flashes of light and his eyes shine and sparkle like the coming of daylight (41:18); his breath looks like fire (41:19); the source of his strength is in his powerful neck (41:22); his flesh defies penetration (41:23); and he has a heart of stone (41:24).

What awesome metaphors descriptive of evil! Yes, the ugly crocodile in its own way is an odd combination of strength, tenacity, gracefulness, and power, but as God warns Job, we dare not attempt to capture, tame, trust, or play with a crocodile (41:1–7). We cannot handle a crocodile on our own because we will always come out the loser.

Then to further give color to the picture, God tells Job that to attempt to subdue the crocodile is futile because swords, spears, darts, javelins, arrows, and slingstones—all devices in Job's day for overcoming a powerful enemy—would be useless and would merely cause him to laugh (41:26–29).

But that isn't all. God isn't through yet, for now He goes on to caution against even making a crocodile angry—an aroused crocodile is like an angered devil. He makes the deep water churn and boil like

The Job writer tells us that after Job's confrontation with God and his repentance through the Lord's special grace and mercy, Job once again became the owner of vast herds of sheep and goats. It wasn't that Job, even with his repentance, had earned or deserved the restoration of his livestock. Rather, we have evidence in this story of the extent of God's grace.

a large pot or caldron, he churns up the sea or river and makes it seethe like a pot of oil or ointment (41:31), and he leaves a great glistening trail or wake in the water (41:32).

What a picture of power and anger! Certainly, no other animal is quite like the crocodile who attacks without provocation and fights without fear. He is indeed a stark symbol of evil. Then the Lord closes out His remarks by saying in picture language that Job would have understood so well, "he is king of all the children of pride" (41:34).

A Child of Pride

A man of Job's wisdom and insight would have gotten the message immediately as a fatal blow had been struck to his pride. He had demanded that God prove that He is just and fair by acting swiftly and surely against evil. But now he realizes that his pride has put him on the side of evil even though he hadn't been guilty of moral sin. Now he saw that if God were to act swiftly against evil, he, too, would be a victim of God's justice.

Once again we learn from the Job story. Like Job, we tend to classify evil. We label murder or stealing as gross evil, but we take a different attitude toward gossip or cheating on our income tax. We would label character assassination as evil but not hesitate to make snide remarks about another person's looks or manner of dress. Like Job we would rationalize pride as beneficial and our right. And like Job, we become upset if God doesn't strike out quickly against anything and anyone we regard as evil. We, too, seem to take satisfaction in setting ourselves up to play God.

A Question of Trust

Although God has not responded directly to Job's original question, "Why do I suffer?" He has posed the larger and more important question, "Whom do you trust?" Job's righteousness and material wealth had lulled him into a state of spiritual self-sufficiency. And his suffering had pushed him to the brink of blasphemy as he doubted God's wisdom, power, justice, and love.

So, to help bring him to his senses God spoke to him out of the whirlwind. Question after unanswered question moved Job back to the basics of faith. He began to understand that God alone had the power to create the universe, the wisdom to run it, and the love to care for it. And he began to understand that he can—and must—trust God. God knows what He is doing in permitting evil to exist. And He will act according to His eternal purposes at the right time. Although this means that suffering becomes a part of human existence, God's grace enables us to handle whatever happens.

Paul, that great apostle to the gentiles, came to

understand this clearly when he begged for relief from his "thorn in the flesh." The answer from the same God who talked with Job was straightforward and simple as God said, "My grace is sufficient for thee" (2 Cor. 12:7–9).

Job Repents (42:1–6)

It is decision time for Job. Having confessed his pride, can he now confess his complete trust in God? Can he trust in the *person* of God without receiving an answer to his "Why?" Can he believe in the *power* of God when Satan remains free to work evil in the world? Can he trust in the *promise* of God to give him grace for every circumstance, including his suffering? In summary, can Job trust in a God who will give him no promise of immunity from the accidents of nature, from the actions of evil men, and from the attacks of Satan? In other words, can Job trust God and serve Him for no other reason than love?

Job's Leap of Faith

Now, Job takes the great leap of faith as he affirms his higher and larger level of trust in God. As of this moment he affirms without question, "I know that thou canst do every thing, and that no thought can be withholden from thee [none of Your plans can be blocked or defeated]" (42:2).

Next, Job refers back to the first question God put to him (38:2), and then he admits frankly that he has confronted "things too wonderful for me" (42:3). God's ways exceed anything the human mind can imagine! Job no longer feels self-sufficient; he has put himself into the hands of God with complete confidence in His power, wisdom, and love. He has had a life-changing personal encounter with God.

I am always intrigued by tonal words, words that set the tone or mood of a chapter or book. From the very beginning of the Book of Job, the word *fear* has been the tonal word to describe Job's relationship with God. Even though God refers to him as "My servant," Job's earlier creed of faith is still summed up in the words, "The *fear* of the Lord is the beginning of wisdom" (italics mine).

But now a new tonal word has crept into Job's vocabulary as he confesses that he has talked without understanding about "things too wonderful for me." *Wonderful* is a child's word. It expresses the wild-eyed anticipation and excitement of a child exploring the wonders of the seashore or a cave along the river.

To approach the Lord with fear is one level of faith; to approach Him with wonder is a grander and more glorious level. After this experience Job will never again cower in fear or prance into God's presence like a prince before a king. Rather, he will move into the presence of the Lord with awe mingled with anticipation—the essence of wonder. Now, Job has learned to worship as well as trust.

Job's Magnificent Confession

We come now to one of the greatest statements in all of the Job story. We have agonized with him as he has wrestled with the "Why?" of all that has happened to him. He is the ancient illustration of the question, "Why do bad things happen to good people?" We have listened to his intellectual descriptions of his faith and belief in God. In this he has not been much different from Eliphaz, Bildad, and Zophar, except his God is a bit more personal than theirs.

But something has happened, and he now makes his magnificent confession, "I have heard of thee by the hearing of the ear: but now mine eye seeth thee" (42:5). In His earlier words, God had spoken to Job in symbols. Now Job uses symbols of his own as he draws the distinction between "hearing of the ear" and the "seeing of the eye."

As we learned earlier, the "ear" is used in Scripture to symbolize human reason. It is true that reason is a part of the image of God in us—but only a part. The use of reason is a way in which we discover truth—but only one of the ways. Job admits that before his suffering and before God spoke to him he had relied exclusively on reason for his understanding of God. Consequently, for Job, God had remained at a distance as an abstract concept.

Now, however, Job wants God to know that he "sees" Him with his eye—the biblical symbol of spiritual insight that floods our beings and changes how we feel and what we do, as well as the way we think. Jesus used the symbol of the eye in the same way when He said, "The light of the body is the eye: if therefore thine eye be single, thy whole body shall be full of light" (Matt. 6:22).

Job is witness to a grand transformation when he tells God, "Now mine eye seeth thee." Intellectually, he had felt an earlier flash of insight into the mind and heart of God when he sang, "For I know that my redeemer liveth, and that he shall stand at the latter day upon the earth: And though after my skin worms destroy this body, yet in my flesh shall I see God" (19:25–26).

True, these words were the turning point in Job's spiritual journey through suffering. But his greater experience is reserved for the moment when his faith floods his total being and his relationship with God becomes one of complete trust. Now, with his emotions and will as well as his intellect he can say, "Though he slay me yet will I trust in him."

As a hospital chaplain, I learned that patients who refused to acknowledge their illness or resigned themselves to its fate hindered the healing process. Frequently, doctors asked me to assist in leading such patients toward a change of attitude. Not unlike the reactions of Job, we often heard cries of anger and bitterness followed by rationalizations for guilt and negotiations with God—"If You'll heal me, I'll . . ."

Step-by-step through those moments of struggle I would stick by the patient, always listening, sometimes praying, and occasionally quoting a promise from Scripture. Finally, as a rule, there would come a moment of acceptance when a sense of peace settled over the patient who would then in his or her own words repeat a version of "Though he slay me, yet will I trust in him." The healing of trust began, not always with survival, but always with peace. This is the meaning of Job's confession, "But now mine eye seeth thee."

Of course, none of us can see the Person of God or stand in His presence without realizing how weak and sinful we are. We're not surprised, then, when Job bows low and says, "I abhor myself," and repents with dust and ashes on his head (42:6). But both the man and the situation have changed. Under the dust and ashes that cover a blackened and scaly bag of bones there is a gleam in his eye.

Father, I can say with Job, my eye seeth thee. *Before, I had heard of You, but now, I know You for myself.* AMEN.

WHAT THIS SCRIPTURE MEANS TO ME
Job 38:1—42:6

The subject was healing and prayer, and the opinions and experiences of the well-dressed Sunday school class members bounced back and forth across the room.

"Well, this is what I think . . ." declared one particularly opinionated young woman.

"I think that is baloney!" offered another strong voice.

"I prayed, and my grandmother got well," stated a new Christian in the group. "But then I prayed for my father, and he died."

I let the conversation go on for a few moments, eager to allow the Spirit enough freedom and space to teach us. All the time, however, I was keenly aware of my young friend who sat in a wheelchair.

"What must she be feeling?" I wondered to myself, remembering the years of prayers that had been offered on her behalf. "How does she hear all of this after all she has been through?"

I thought back on the early days of Debbie's illness, back when she was still up on her feet and able to take care of herself and her two young sons. I recalled the progressive nature of her disease as the slow, insidious illness had coiled itself through her body, robbing her bit by bit of her abilities.

A faint smile played around her mouth. Calmly and quietly, she listened to each pronouncement. Never did she jump to refute their words. She simply listened.

By her side sat Corky, Debbie's husband. He, too, took it all in, never jumping to defend God or offer platitudes. Finally, however, he spoke.

"It's true that we may never be healed on this side of heaven," he began, and I sensed with my whole body the shifting of the mood in the room.

It was as if we were holding a collective breath, for, suddenly, the reality of our wheelchair-bound friend got our attention. This word, spoken by the one who had walked alongside his suffering wife for most of their marriage, carried authority. He who had had youthful dreams nipped in the bud by multiple sclerosis knew what he was talking about. This man, caught in the tangled web of ever-increasing medical bills, could tell us all about expecting miracles and pleading with God for a reprieve.

"Our prayers may not be answered like we want them to be," the young husband continued, "but that doesn't mean we have to live like victims in the meantime."

I hadn't really planned on reaching any conclusions that morning. To tell the truth, I had prepared the lesson with a bit of frustration, for the teachings about prayer and healing always leave me a little frustrated. Given the unanswerable questions, I feel so inept as a teacher.

Unable to draw things to a tidy conclusion, I had planned on leaving my learners to grapple with the questions themselves. To reassure them that this questioning back and forth between Creator and creature was nothing new, I might even have challenged them with God's words to Job, "Where wast thou when I laid the foundations of the earth? declare if thou hast understanding?"

Little did I know or expect that the quiet witness of true veterans would be the vehicle of God's grace. Who was to guess that such few words could expose Mystery so eloquently?

I haven't been able to get away from the power of Corky's words or Debbie's silent witness. Nor have I been able to shake the impact of their answer to a question I thought was unanswerable. The answer is in the "Who," and the Who is God.

LESSON 8
JOB 42:7–17

Remembering Job: Man of Grace

Father, Thank You for reminding me that my sometimes frazzled, fragmented, split-into-ten-different-directions life is made wonderfully whole by Your grace. Help me to tap into Your grace today, Lord. AMEN.

Job is still on the ash heap, but there is a difference. No longer is he attesting to his innocence, declaring his righteousness, and demanding that God justify his suffering. Instead, he bows in the Presence of the Holy, confesses his unworthiness, repents of his pride, affirms his trust, and is reconciled with God. Even though he is still on the ash heap, grace has made him whole.

The Gift of Grace

The Book of Job is classified as wisdom literature in the Bible. It is also a book of prophecy. Although thousands of years would pass before the coming of Jesus Christ, Job's story promises our redemption from sin and our reconciliation with God through the gift of grace.

By definition, grace is "unmerited favor." It cannot be earned, bought, or inherited. Through suffering, Job had learned to trust in God rather than in his own righteousness. When he did, grace flooded his soul, and he was healed, even with dust and ashes on his head.

John Wesley, the father of Methodism, is another

example of a man who tried to become "perfect" in righteousness through self-discipline. From his earliest childhood, his mother taught him to fear God and shun evil. Later, in his university days at Oxford, he and his brother Charles formed "The Holy Club" with rigid rules and rigorous accountability as the condition for membership. Their search for righteousness was so lock-step that their fellow students mocked them as "Methodists."

But in spite of all the discipline and the following of rules, holiness of heart continued to elude Wesley even after he received appointment as an Oxford don, was ordained as an Anglican priest, and commissioned as a missionary to America.

Wesley's spiritual self-discipline would shame most of us who live self-indulgent lives today. Yet, he never found the assurance of salvation until he went reluctantly to a little chapel on Aldersgate Street in London where someone was reading from Luther's Preface to the Epistle to the Romans. When the reader came to the words describing faith as the divine work of God in us and totally independent of good works, Wesley said, "I felt my heart strangely warmed. I felt I did trust in Christ, and Christ alone, for salvation; and an assurance was given to me that He had taken away my sins, even mine, and saved me from the law of sin and death."

In that moment Wesley not only discovered the *meaning* of grace, he experienced the *gift* of grace. When he testified, "I felt I did trust in Christ, and Christ alone, for salvation," he junked a lifetime of spiritual discipline and good works in his search for true righteousness. From then on, he and his brother Charles sang and preached the message of grace as "free in all, and free for all" until England was spiritually revolutionized. No hymn of Charles Wesley carries the theme of their ministry better than

> O for a thousand tongues to sing
> My great Redeemer's praise,
> The glories of my God and King,
> The triumphs of His grace!

Wesley at Aldersgate and Job on an ash heap are companions in grace.

The Test of Grace
(42:7–9)

Nothing more needs to be said to Job. God and His servant are completely reconciled, the lines of communication are open, and their relationship is deeper and closer than ever before. So, God now turns to Job's three friends and speaks directly to Eliphaz, the eldest.

Honesty or Hypocrisy?

It is God's turn to be angry (42:7). Eliphaz, Bildad, and Zophar had taken it upon themselves to defend His character and define His Truth. Now, mincing no words, God tells Eliphaz, ". . . for ye have not spoken of me the thing that is right [you haven't said the right things about Me] as my servant Job hath" (42:7).

Who knows the mind of God? Humanly speaking, it seems as if Eliphaz, Bildad, and Zophar argued honestly on behalf of God's wisdom, power, and justice. It was Job who ranted and raved that God was unfair and didn't even know what He was doing, or didn't care, or couldn't do anything about it. Why then did God get angry at the three friends rather than Job?

We have a critical distinction here. Eliphaz, Bildad, and Zophar from all outward appearance had defended God and His truth, but in reality they were protecting their own egos and their own interpretation of truth. In a word, they were the Pharisees of Job's day. As with the Pharisees, Eliphaz, Bildad, and Zophar focused on a narrow and static doctrine of justice which they wielded like a club in condemning Job.

We've already mentioned the saying, "If Satan cannot keep us from righteousness, he will try to make us self-righteous." This related saying is also true, "If Satan cannot keep us from the truth, he will try to get us to defend a half-truth." The doctrine of justice which Eliphaz, Bildad, and Zophar believed in so strongly wasn't wrong until they made it a rigid and closed religious system which limited new spiritual insight and stunted their faith.

Job may have been guilty of self-righteousness, but Eliphaz and his friends were guilty of hypocrisy.

And by strict definition, hypocrisy means misrepresenting God either by our words or our actions.

Evidently, nothing disturbs God more than when He is used as an excuse for judging and oppressing people. Job, at least, protested his suffering in all honesty and didn't blame anybody else for what was happening to him. In so many words, he told his friends, "The argument is between God and me." As I reflect on God's reaction of anger with Eliphaz and His acceptance of Job in our Scripture lesson, it seems to me that it is not likely that God is offended by our honesty, but He most certainly rejects our hypocrisy.

Our Job writer now tells us that God gave Eliphaz, Bildad, and Zophar some specific instructions. They are told to take seven bulls and seven rams and sacrifice them as a burnt offering in behalf of themselves. But that isn't all. They are to ask Job to pray for them because God tells them He will hear Job's prayers but not theirs. And three times during this sequence God refers to Job as "My servant." After their long self-righteous tirades against Job, it must have been more than a little humiliating to be required to ask Job to pray for them.

Throughout Job's extended period of suffering from the loss of family, material wealth, and health, all of which had exposed his pride and had taken him more than once to the border of blasphemy, the personal and spiritual relationship between Job and God had remained intact. This is a marvelous illustration of the character of God. Even when we struggle in our hard times of suffering, when we question Him, God still wants us to know, "You belong to Me, I love you, and I'm proud of you." In other words, God Himself participates in our suffering even as He participated in Christ's suffering on the cross. At no time was God indifferent to Job's suffering, and at no time can we be indifferent to the suffering of our neighbors across the street or across the world.

It is this quality or attribute of God that over and over again in the Psalms is referred to as His mercy. For example, the Psalmist wrote, "I will be glad and rejoice in thy *mercy*" (Psa. 31:7, italics mine). Actually, the Hebrew word used for "mercy" is an impor-

Justice or Mercy?

153

tant word throughout all of the Old Testament. It is variously translated "mercy" or "love" or "steadfast love" or "loving kindness" or "unfailing love."

The Lord's instruction to ask Job to pray for them has a touch of wonderful irony. Throughout all of the earlier conversations Eliphaz had assumed the role of intercessor on Job's behalf, and he had promised Job that if he would repent and get right with God the Lord might also give him a similar honor. For Eliphaz the role of intercessor was self-appointed. But now, God has turned the tables as He tells Eliphaz that Job will intercede and pray for him and his two friends. This had to be a bitter pill for the three wise men from the East to swallow.

It is wrong to think that our times of suffering and doubt mean a break in our relationship with God. Actually, pain is the price we pay for being alive. As tough as our times of pain and suffering may be, the tougher truth is that we only learn and grow through pain. As a prominent Christian leader once said, "Life is not a matter of winning or losing, but of winning or learning." Elihu had been right—through his suffering Job had learned lessons that he would have missed otherwise.

Speaking of Elihu, he has now disappeared from the scene. God has nothing to say about him and his role as Job's critic and counselor. This is the way it is so often with people who prepare the way for God to speak. They appear briefly on the stage of human history, speak their small part, and then move off the stage into obscurity. As with John the Baptist, their sole purpose is to prepare the way for God. After a fleeting moment on center stage, their parting word echoes that of John the Baptist, "He [Christ] must increase, but I must decrease." Elihu had fulfilled his role as God's preparer of the way, speaking with the "Spirit of understanding" through the "breath of the Almighty."

Grace received, grace given. That is the spirit of people who have seen God and received His love. Jesus is our example. After He taught us to love our enemies, He showed us the meaning of His words on the cross when He spoke so graciously, "Father, forgive them; for they know not what they do" (Luke 23:34).

When Job prayed for his friends, two things happened. First, Eliphaz, Bildad, and Zophar were restored in their relationship with God. And then all of Job's losses were restored to him double—health and wealth, fame and family.

The Restoration of Grace (42:10)

Some Old Testment critics feel that the restoration of Job's health, wealth, fame and family cancels out the value of the Book of Job. They argue that God restored Job to prosperity because of his repentance, thereby confirming the belief of Job's friends that sin produces suffering and repentance produces prosperity. Also, they argue that Job's restoration proves that Satan was right when he sneered, "Doth Job fear God for nought [nothing]?" (1:9). But to think that way is to fail to understand the meaning of grace.

According to this part of our Scripture lesson, Job's losses were not restored after his repentance but after his intercession. His prayer for his three friends-turned-critics is linked with his restoration by the conjunction *and:* "And the Lord turned the captivity of Job [restored Job's losses], when he prayed for his friends" (42:10).

The Meaning of Grace

It is God's grace that makes the difference. Job still sat on the ash heap after his repentance. He had no assurance that he would ever be healed physically or restored to prosperity. Yet, having given up all claim to self-sufficiency and having confessed his total trust in God, he had peace of mind and soul. With the assurance of grace, nothing more is needed.

Remember that Job never lost his reputation as a man of integrity. In fact, he had passed the most severe test of character after he was accused of sin—secret sin, social sin, and the sins of the rich and famous. Not one single accusation could be held against him. And then he received the grace of God.

In the Job story we see demonstrated the spiritual traits that distinguished Jesus Christ as a person who was "full of grace and truth" (John 1:14). The divine

The Attitude of Grace

fusion of grace and truth which makes Jesus so desirable to us has become the rare quality which puts Job far beyond his earlier reputation for being righteous and wise. To be righteous, avoid evil, and fear God is good, but to be full of grace and truth is both better and best.

Without minimizing the fact that God Himself restored Job's losses with a doubling of his blessings, we can be sure that it was Job's new attitude toward God, himself, and others that speeded his restoration. He made his first fortune by doing business as a man of integrity in a land of cut-throat competition; he gains his second fortune by being a man of truth and grace in a land where such a blend of integrity and compassion was rare, if not unknown.

The Hospitality of Grace (42:11)

Integrity deals with truth; grace deals with people. As we noted earlier, we show that we have received grace when we in turn show grace to others.

Job's second test of grace comes after he is restored to health and wealth, fame and family. "Then"—another key connecting word which indicates that one event is triggered by another—all of Job's brothers, sisters, and friends who had abandoned him during his time of humiliation and suffering appear at his doorstep. They have come to eat with him bearing gifts of silver and gold. After the trouble is over, Job's brothers, sisters, and friends comfort and console him "over all the evil [troubles] that the Lord had brought upon him" (42:11).

The Code of Hospitality

Hospitality ranked near the top of the unwritten code in the culture of the ancient East. Because survival in their wild and treacherous environment was a common need among the people of Uz, they put a premium on entertaining strangers and even aliens who came to their door. Job's friends-turned-critics had accused him of being inhospitable to strangers—either turning them away or giving them leftovers for food. But Job had refuted their accusation by insisting, "The stranger did not lodge in the street: but I opened my doors to the traveller" (31:32). Furthermore, Job insisted that he went the extra mile by pleading the case of strangers in a court of law (29:16).

Justice underlaid the code of hospitality for the land of the ancient East. Everyone became a stranger as they traveled across the long and lonely stretches of desert. As the code of justice dictated "an eye for an eye," the code of hospitality ruled "a meal for a meal and a bed for a bed."

Grace beyond the Code

Nothing in the code of hospitality, however, said anything about brothers, sisters, and friends who abandon you in your difficult times of suffering and then return to curry your favor when you regain your status. Personally, I always feel terribly violated when I know I'm being wooed by people whose motives are transparent. Sugar-coated words and syrupy smiles fail to cover up their selfishness. It is obvious that such people are using you to achieve their purposes.

I recall visiting my congressman for the first time. We were friends before his election, and I anticipated renewing our friendship in his new setting. He received me with a flurry, introduced me to his staff, and invited me to lunch in the Congressional Dining Room. As we ate, I noticed that his eyes roamed the room, looking for influential people to whom he could call by name with the obvious intent to impress me. Then, getting impatient with the amount of time we had spent together, he concluded the lunch by asking, "Now, what do you want me to do for you?" His question sickened me. I wanted nothing but his friendship. How quickly he had been spoiled in the corridors of power!

Job's brothers, sisters, and friends came back to him with this same corrupt motive. Simple justice would have sent them away with these words ringing in their ears, "Where were you when I needed you?" Instead, Job showed them the hospitality of grace. It goes far beyond the code of entertaining strangers to the gift of welcoming prodigal people and accepting them even though they may deserve nothing but disdain.

As we read about the celebration at Job's house, we

can see a parallel to a New Testament parable. The prodigal son left his father, wasted his inheritance, indulged in gross sin, and ended up scrapping with pigs over empty husks. When the young man came to his senses, he returned to his father's house expecting to be treated like one of the servants. But his father had been anxiously waiting for him, and when he saw him in the distance, ran to meet him, welcomed his wayward boy home, and threw a huge welcome home party for him.

But the young man's older brother heard the noise of the party with anger. He grumbled about the injustice of celebrating his brother's return when he had never been treated to a party, even though he had stayed home and served his father faithfully on the family farm. In response to his complaint, his father answered, "It was meet [right] that we should make merry, and be glad [have a celebration]: for this thy brother was dead, and is alive again; and was lost, and is found" (Luke 15:32). Only pure and unadulterated grace could say that.

It was this spirit that Job had caught in his confrontation with God. There was no room left in his heart for recrimination against the family and friends who had deserted him. The grace of God calls for celebration of life, not for retaliation against wrong.

Blessings Multiplied (42:12–15)

Next, the Job writer goes into some detail as he describes in broad brush strokes what happened now, "So the Lord blessed the latter end of Job more than his beginning [the end of his life more than the early part]: for he had fourteen thousand sheep, and six thousand camels, and a thousand yoke of oxen, and a thousand she asses [donkeys]. He had also seven sons and three daughters. And he called the name of the first [daughter], Jemima; and the name of the second [daughter], Kezia; and the name of the third [daughter], Keren-happuch" (42:12–14).

Job was blessed with seven sons. The number seven in the Bible signifies perfection—it was the perfect number for Job's inheritance.

It is significant that the Job writer devotes more space and detail to the three daughters. While the seven sons remain nameless, we are given the names

Except for the paved road and the shepherd's modern clothing, this could be a scene in Job's time. The location for this picture is on the ancient King's Highway, a trade route which Job likely traveled.

of the daughters and are told that they were the most beautiful women in all the land (42:15a). Incidently, since their father Job wasn't doing the writing, we can assume the writer reported accurately. As the proud father of daughters, I know that mine are the most beautiful in "all the land," and I don't hesitate one moment to brag about them. Of course, since I'm their father, I suppose my judgment is slanted—even though it is 100 percent true!

In addition, the meaning of their names is most descriptive and certainly validates the judgment of the writer. Jemima means "turtledove," the songbird with the sweetest song in the ancient East. Kezia means "cinnamon," the most precious spice in the ancient East. And Keren-happuch means "horn of paint," the ancient cosmetic case associated with the beauty of the women.

Because of my feelings for my daughters, I believe I can identify with Job just a little bit. But Job had a special reason for being proud of his daughters. Remember, he had a disfiguring and loathesome disease that had forced him into quarantine on an ash heap outside the city walls that had likely made him the butt of jokes for the rowdy kids who happened along. I'm sure after God had given him a new family that every time Job looked at his daughters he saw in their beauty the symbol of God's grace.

Mother of Beauty

There's another dimension of grace here that shouldn't be overlooked. While Job's wife isn't mentioned in this part of the story, daughters need mothers as well as fathers. Perhaps a gift of grace was given to Job's wife in the beauty of her daughters. Although earlier she had urged Job to curse God and die, there is no indication that she abandoned her husband. So, without too much of a stretch of the imagination it is possible that the seven sons and three daughters were a sign of whatever forgiveness was needed between Job and his wife or between God and Job's wife.

The Code of Inheritance

All of our conjecture, however, pales before the fact that Job gave his daughters an inheritance in addition to the inheritance allotted to their brothers. (42:15b). Now, it would be easy to pass over this brief comment and not attach any significance to it. But that would be a mistake, because it gives us insight into the emerging sensitivity of Job, and it also tells us that Job's pride has undergone a spiritual experience.

Men ruled society and families in the ancient East. Women were looked upon as commodities to be bought and sold, as baby-makers to bear sons, and as second-class citizens without voice or vote. Patriarchal and sexist attitudes controlled society life then and for centuries to come. Even when Moses received the Law of God, the standard for passing down the family inheritance provided for daughters only if there were no sons to claim their rights.

But Job broke the code of culture, the laws of the land, and the expectations of people when he gave his daughters equal shares, along with their brothers, of the family inheritance. Legally, they had nothing coming. Yet when their father left them a full share of his wealth, they received a gift of grace.

At one time Job believed that he was entitled to his blessings because of his special relationship with God, but that was no longer true. When Job repented of his pride on the ash heap, he knew that God didn't owe him anything. His blessings came only through God's grace. It isn't surprising, then, that when it came time for him to distribute his inheritance, he remembered the grace of God and gave his daughters an equal share.

Grace beyond the Code

There is an analogy in all of this that is profoundly important. As non-Jews—gentiles—we identify with Job's daughters. Job's sons symbolize the people of Israel who were considered the natural heirs of God's salvation. On the other hand, the daughters symbolize gentiles—people without a name or nation who were considered without rights spiritually.

Centuries before the time when the Apostle Peter arrived at what for him was a shocking conclusion—that Christ died for *everyone,* not just for Jews—Job modeled God's grace for the world. In the Apostle Paul's letter to the Christians at Rome, gentiles are compared to wild olive shoots that have been grafted in among the natural branches and share equally in the nourishment that comes through the root. Then to this vivid picture of grace, Paul adds the warning, "Boast not against the branches [Don't be proud because you are just a branch]. . . . For if God spared not the natural branches, take heed lest he also spare not thee [if God didn't spare the natural branches, the Jews, He won't spare you either]" (Rom. 11:18–21). This simply means that by His grace God included us, and we celebrate that grace by giving grace to others without limit.

One more gift of grace is given to Job (42:16). We're told now that he lived one hundred and forty

The Tribute of Grace (42:16–17)

years longer and realized his dream of seeing four generations of children and grandchildren. What more could he ask? As a father and grandfather whose children live at a distance, I find myself desperately missing the moments of celebration with them—the first tooth, the first step, birthday parties, holiday meals, sports events, and worshiping in the family pew. So, at the slightest provocation or invitation, my wife and I travel across the country to "dip into" the life of our family. Every minute together is cherished as a gift of grace. Of all human relationships, Job suffered most when he lost his children. God knew this and saved the greatest blessing for the last. Job's restoration was complete when, once again, he could enjoy the richness of having his children with him (29:5–6).

A Long and Full Life

"So Job died, being old and full of days" (42:17). His epitaph is simple, but significant. As a reminder that the mortality rate for human beings is still 100 percent, Job died. The grace of God did not save him from death, but it helped him die well. Even in his death there is the footnote that gives us a clue to the quality of his life. He died, "full of days."

At first, we might assume that "full of days" refers to his longevity. But, it could also refer to the quality of Job's life. If so, it means that he lived to the fullest every day until he died. Some people limp through their days more dead than alive. They have no joy and make others miserable.

Other people are so intent on the future that they miss the fullness of the moment. I am one of those people. Almost every day, I catch myself anticipating what's ahead rather than discovering the richness of the "now." But when I do stop long enough to take what the present moment offers, life fills up with peace and joy. I learn what Jesus meant when he promised, "I am come that they might have life, and that they might have it more abundantly" (John 10:10).

To live fully each day of our lives is a gift of grace. We do not fret about the past because grace covers our sins. We are not anxious about the future because grace is promised a day at a time. We can live as Job lived and die as Job died, "full of days."

Job was introduced as a man "perfect" in righteousness. We will remember him as a man "full" of grace.

Savior, You are the abundant life! Because I really know You I can live each day in the refreshing, renewing strength of the Holy Spirit. Fill me up with Your joy and let it overflow to those around me. AMEN.

WHAT THIS SCRIPTURE MEANS TO ME
Job 42:7—17

"Why me?" I pouted, pounding the pavement with my self-pity.

"Why me?" I raged, roaring around the house, venting my frustration on anyone who got in my way. "I didn't ask for this!"

"Why me?" I whined, wheeling around the corner in my puffed-up pomposity, thinking I was alone so that I could say whatever I chose.

"You never ask that when you get the good stuff," my child sniffed.

Stopped in my tracks, I stared in disbelief. Big brown eyes stared back at me. Those eyes held no guile; clear, clean truth had exposed me to myself. She, recognizing that perhaps she had scraped my soft spot, turned around and headed in the opposite direction.

I plopped down in my chair, thunderstruck. Looking back, I was too overwhelmed with the profundity of my child's remark to be angry or ashamed that she'd caught me in the throes of self-pity.

In the quiet, I saw myself brand new, and what I saw, I didn't particularly like. Familiar with those breakthrough moments, though, I made up my mind to listen to the discomfort and see through to new insight. I decided to tell myself the truth, no matter how painful it was to be.

Like Job, I had my vision cleared all of a sudden. I remembered his words to God, and smiled to myself, "I have heard of thee by the hearing of the ear: but now mine eye seeth thee." My child was the one who had scraped the fog away.

It was true, I saw, that I accept the good stuff of life as if it were mine by divine right. I demand mercy for myself, but I want justice for others. I become trapped in self-absorption, thinking my pain is the best of all pains. Surely I hurt more than anyone else. I have more burdens, more responsibilities, more disadvantages. When I am at my worst, I know that I am the most special sufferer of all. I can get downright proud of the uniqueness of my difficulty!

It's easy to get enmeshed in dark grandiosity. Thinking that my problems are unique and different is a common tendency and part of the pain of being human. To move out of that position requires an act of the will and a decision to join the human race in accepting the fact that life is tough for all of us.

I wish I could tell you that my daughter's quiet confrontation brought me to deep humility and repentance. Instead, my stubborn will fought the truth and resisted change with a fierceness of passion reserved for bloody battles.

Neither was I able once and for all to lay down my deep preoccupation with myself. Instead, moving beyond myself to acceptance of life's realities comes with baby steps forward and giant leaps backward. Bit by bit, however, as I look back over the long haul, I can see the fingerprints of God's grace placed all over my life.

As I am becoming able to lay down my self-centeredness, I am also able to give to others the gift of my concern and the cleanness of free love, with fewer and fewer constraints. More and more, I am able to give out of the overflow of what God has done in me rather than giving in order to get the other person to love me. Gradually, I am accepting the bounty of God's grace, awestruck by His goodness, and that gratitude somehow gives me the strength to turn the searchlight off myself and bathe others with concern and compassion.

Little by little, like Job, I am learning about the One who stands behind all my questions, accepting His grace and love, and then passing it along to someone who just may be hurting as much as I!

Index

References to illustrations are given in italics.

A NOTE TO THE READER

This original Guideposts book is brought to you by the same editors who prepare *Guideposts*, a monthly magazine filled with true stories of people's adventures in faith.

If you have found inspiration in this book, we think you'll find monthly help and inspiration in the exciting stories that appear in our magazine.

Guideposts is not sold on the newsstand. It's available by subscription only. And subscribing is easy. All you have to do is write Guideposts Associates, Inc., Carmel, New York 10512. A year's subscription costs only $8.95 in the United States, $10.95 in Canada and overseas.

When you subscribe, each month you can count on receiving exciting new evidence of God's presence and His abiding love for His people.